AGRARIAN BRITAIN 1700-1980

Simon Mason

GENERAL EDITOR **Jon Nicho**

Contents

Basil Blackwell

First published 1984

© Simon Mason 1984

Reprinted 1985, 1986, 1987

ISBN 0 631 91420 X

Typesetting by Getset (BTS) Ltd, Eynsham, Oxford
Designed by Sue Richards
Printed in Hong Kong by Wing King Tong Co. Ltd.

BLACKWELL HISTORY PROJECT

The First World War
The Second World War
The United States of America
Russia
Germany
The Great Power Conflict after 1945
International Relations, 1919-39

Agrarian Britain 1700-1980
The Industrial Revolution
Transport and Communications 1750-1980
Trade Unions and Social Reform
Social Problems 1760-1980

History of Medicine
The Irish Question
The Middle East
Source Book: How to use Evidence

Acknowledgements

Verses from *The Battery Hen* by Pam Ayres are reproduced by kind permission of the Hutchinson Publishing Group Ltd Aerofilms Limited 5(D); Bedfordshire County Council 19(E); BBC Hulton Picture Library 7(G), 9(E), 12(A) (D), 13(F), 23(E), 28(C), 32(A), 48(A), 53(E), 56(B), 57(D); Courtesy of the Trustees of the British Museum 7(E), 15(G), 26(E); Cambridge University Press (*The Rural Revolution in an English Village* by Roy Sturgess) 18(A), 20(B), 29(D); Dartington Rural Archive 46(B), 47(E), 50(E); E P Publishing Limited 54(C); *The Farmers' Weekly* 59(F); The Fotomas Index: Introduction; Institute of Agricultural History and Museum of English Rural Life, University of Reading 36(B), 52(B) and Cover; Longman Group Limited 16(A); Macdonald and Co Limited (*Incredible Century* by R J Unstead) 56(A); The Mansell Collection 6(B), 8(B), 9(C), 14(B) (C), 22(A), 33(F), 34(B), 37(C), 39(E), 43(E), 44(B), 48(B); Mary Evans Picture Library 24(A), 35(C), 42(A); National Farmers' Union 60(B); Nuffield College, Oxford 45(C); Packer's Studio, Chipping Norton 61(D); Royal Agricultural Society of England 61(E); The Science Museum 10(B), 11(C); Trades Union Congress 30(A).

Introduction

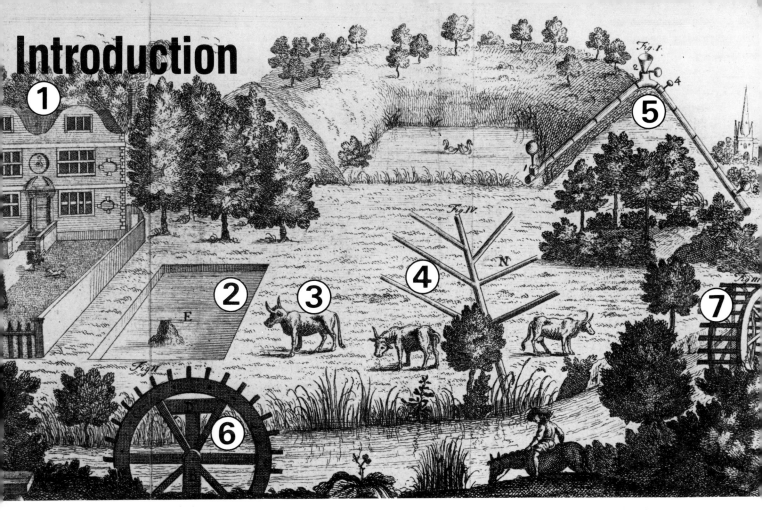

If you were to make a list of the five most important industries in Britain today, which industries would you write down?

In the 1980s, so many people live in towns that we tend to forget that agriculture is still one of our most important industries. About 650 000 people, or 2.6% of the working population, have jobs in agriculture. It is the industry which produces over half our food, although today many tons of produce are imported.

Many people still think of farms and villages as quiet places where farmers and farm-workers lead tranquil lives. In fact modern farming is nothing like this. Many farms are run like big businesses and the people who own them are anxious to make lots of money. New machines and techniques make modern farms busy, often noisy places to work in. Farmers have so many machines that fewer farm labourers are needed than ever before; in 1974 there were twice as many farm labourers as in 1984. Yet in 1984, with less land being farmed and fewer farm workers, more food is being produced. New crops, breeds of animals and machines have made this possible.

In this book you will find out how agriculture, the oldest industry in the world, has changed over the past 280 years. Each chapter contains historical *evidence* to enable you to work out what happened for yourself. There are maps, photographs, diagrams and statistics to help you. Once you have finished the book, you may be able to look at farms, fields, animals, crops and buildings in a different way.

The picture on this page is a piece of historical evidence. It is an illustration from a book written in 1727 called *A Complete Body of Husbandry* by Richard Brandley. Study the evidence for a few minutes and then try to answer the questions.

??????????????????

1 What can you see at points **1 – 7**?

2 What sources of power were used on this farm?

3 Do you think this is a picture of a real farm? Give reasons for your answer.

4 What message was the artist trying to give a person looking at the picture? (Clue: Look at the book's title.)

5 How would a modern farm differ from the farm in the picture?

1 The Open-Field Village

A Areas of England and Wales with open-field farms in 1700-1800

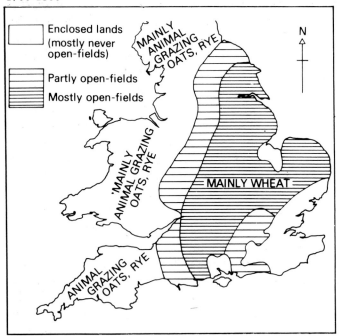

From Norman times until about 1700 most of the villages in the Midlands, the South of England and East Anglia were surrounded by huge 'open' fields. Map **A** shows where these open-field villages were situated.

They were called 'open' fields because there were no hedges or fences in them. Each large field was divided into strips which were shared out among the village people according to the amount of land they owned or rented. The strips varied in size and shape but were usually about half a hectare (one acre) in area, as much as a man could plough in a day. The strips were separated from each other by unploughed ridges of soil called *balks*.

The Domesday Book of 1086 AD has this entry about a village in Nottinghamshire:

' *In Laxintune* (Laxton) *there is land for six ploughs. Walter, Geoffrey Alselin's man, has one plough and there are twenty-two villagers and seven smallholders who have five ploughs. There are five male slaves and one female slave. The value in the time of King Edward the Confessor was £9; it is now worth £6.* ' **(B)**

Today Laxton is worth about £2 million and there are no slaves. The number of villagers owning or renting land is about the same as in 1086. The most surprising thing about Laxton is that the village uses the same system of farming as in 1086. No other village in Britain still uses this method to produce its food. **C** shows what Laxton looks like today. **D** is an aerial photograph of the village, and in the lower part of the picture you can see some of the strips which divide the fields. Surrounding Laxton were four great open fields which were used for *arable* farming. This means the fields were used to grow wheat, oats or barley.

In each large field, farmers followed the same system of farming. Every year, one field was left fallow (to rest so that the soil could recover its goodness). To keep the soil in good condition, the fallow field had to be kept ploughed. The second field (West Field) was sown with wheat, the third with barley. The following year, the

C A map of Laxton today, showing the four great open fields

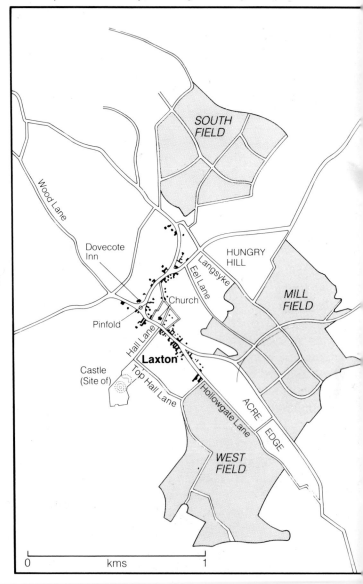

second field would be left fallow, the third field sown with oats and the first field sown with barley. This is known as a system of *crop rotation*. In many parts of Britain this system worked remarkably well. However, it meant that a farmer's holdings were scattered over a wide area and only two-thirds of the land was being used at any one time.

At harvest time, all the villagers would help each other gather in crops. The village worked as a community with several farmers clubbing together to provide horses, carts and labour. Ploughing, sowing and lambing were also organized on a sharing basis. After the harvest, cattle were allowed to graze on the stubble until the land had to be ploughed ready for the next crop.

Beyond the arable land were meadows which the farmers mowed for hay for winter feed. There were also commons and wastelands where the villagers pastured their cattle, geese and sheep. The woodland north of Mill Field and south of South Field provided the villagers of Laxton with free firewood, acorns, berries and timber.

What was it like to work in Laxton in 1700? **E** gives an idea of how a ploughman spent a working day:

❛The plowman shall rise before four o'clock in the morning, and after thanks given to God for his rest, he shall go into his stable or beast house. First, he shall feed his cattle, then clean the house and make the booths clean. Then he shall water both his oxen and horses and give them fodder such as chaff and dry pease.

And while they are eating, he shall make ready his collars, halters and plow-gears . . . till six. Then he shall come into breakfast for half an hour and then another half hour to the yoking and gearing of his cattle . . . and then he shall plough from seven o'clock in the morning till between two or three in the afternoon. Then he shall unyoke his cattle and bring them home; he shall go into his dinner and at four of the clock he shall go to his cattle again and give them more food.

At six of the clock he shall come into supper, and after supper sit by the fireside, mend shoes . . . or else grind malt till it be fully eight of the clock. Then he shall take his candle and go see his cattle and look that they are safely tied. Then, giving God thanks . . . rest till the next morning. ❜ **(E)**

D Laxton from the air

??????????????????

1 The following chart shows a three-field rotation at Laxton between 1702 and 1704. Complete the information on the chart:

Year	Mill Field	South Field	West Field
1702	Fallow	Wheat	Barley
1703	Barley	?	?
1704	?	?	?

Why was the land farmed in this way?

2 It is often stated that open-field farming was wasteful of **a** time; **b** land; **c** labour.
Use the text and the evidence to find reasons for this.

3 Using **C**, work out what you can see at points **1 – 5** in evidence **D**.

4 Using **C** and **D**, draw a detailed map of what you think Laxton probably looked like in 1700. You can assume that the road patterns were the same in the eighteenth century as they are on the modern map.

2 The Farming Community in 1700

B *Mr and Mrs Andrews*, by Thomas Gainsborough

❛ *Sir Roger, the squire, is in charge of the whole congregation. He keeps them in very good order and will not allow anyone to sleep during the church service apart from himself. If, by chance, he has taken a short nap during the sermon, upon recovering out of it, he stands up and looks about him, and if he sees anyone else nodding off, either he wakes them up himself or he sends his servant to them.* ❜ (A)

In 1700, a squire like Sir Roger was the most important person in local farming and the village. He owned a great deal of land and was a Justice of the Peace (a magistrate). **B** is a picture of a young squire and his wife. The squire's home was the hall or manor where he liked to treat his friends to huge meals washed down with plenty of port or ale. He owned a coach and horses but was only able to travel around the village in such grand style in fine weather as many of the roads were little better than farm tracks. His favourite hobbies were fox-hunting and going to race meetings. He liked country sports and might set man-traps and spring guns to try to catch poachers:

❛ *In his youth Sir Roger had shot his way through forty coveys of partridges in a season and tired many a salmon with a line consisting of a single hair. Everyone thanked* him *for his remarkable enmity towards foxes and he destroyed more of these vermin in one year than it was thought the whole country could have produced. His hunting horses were the finest and best managed in all these parts . . . if you do not allow men of landed estates to preserve their game, you could not prevail upon them to reside in the country.* ❜ (C)

Second in importance to the squire was the village parson (or rector) whom the squire often chose for the job. In 1700 far more people went to church than do today and so the parson was at the centre of village life. His house was usually near the church. Living so close to the centre of the village, he knew most of the villagers well. He visited the homes of the poor and whenever possible helped them out with money and food. But as **D** suggests, some parsons were more interested in things other than the well-being of the poor:

❛ *The Rector of Puddletown was a dear, cheery old man, one of the jolly old school. He did his duty according to his own ideas but at heart I think he loved and lived for one thing which was hunting. I remember hearing that on one occasion a funeral had to be kept waiting at a church till his return from a particularly exciting chase.* ❜ (D)

E is a picture of an eighteenth-century parson.

When not looking after his parish or hunting, the parson may have farmed his own plot of land known as the 'glebe'. He also received a tithe (tenth) of the produce of the farmers in his parish. Sometimes his income from the church was so small that he relied upon the glebe and tithes to make ends meet.

Most farmers in a village like Laxton were freeholders or smallholders. The freeholders owned the land they lived and worked on. Smallholders rented land from the squire or from freeholders. Some of the freeholders were quite wealthy and might even live like the squire.

The farm labourers they employed fell into two distinct groups. One group 'lived in' on the farm and were called farm servants. They had the important farm jobs such as bailiff, shepherd or cowman and were paid up to 2 shillings (10p) a day. The other group lived in small cottages with gardens in which they grew a few vegetables and kept a few animals. They were paid 8d to 1s (3p – 5p) a day for working on nearby farms. They would expect to receive more at haymaking and harvest time when their hours of work were longer. At Foxton, in Cambridgeshire, during the harvest a farm labourer would get:

> ❝ *6 a.m.*   *One pint of strong beer, bread and cheese*
> *8 a.m.*   *Breakfast of cold meat and beer*
> *11 a.m.*   *One pint of strong beer, bread and cheese*
> *1 p.m.*   *Dinner. One day roast beef or mutton (pork will not do) and plain pudding. Next day, boiled beef or mutton and plum pudding.*
> *4 p.m.*   *One pint of strong beer*
> *7 p.m.*   *Hot hash or mutton pies* ❞ (**F**)

E A cartoon drawing of an eighteenth-century parson

On the lowest rung of the social ladder were the squatters. They were poor farmers who built shacks on the commons and wastes, grew a few vegetables and kept one or two scraggy cows and goats. Their shacks were rough hovels, built out of any materials available, and they had no legal rights to the land they lived on or farmed. Many of these families were so poor that they had to ask the parish for help in the form of money or food. Others roamed around the area in the hope of picking up casual work for a few pence a day. **G** shows such a family.

G A family of poor squatters

??????????????????

1 Use the evidence and the text to fill in the information in the chart below:

	Home	Food	Income	Leisure
Squire				
Parson				
Farm Servant				
Squatter				

2 Look closely at **B**. It is a famous painting by the artist Thomas Gainsborough.

   a Describe in detail the clothes of the squire and his wife.

   b Describe the appearance of the landscape around them.

   c What sort of people do you think they were?

   d What do you think Thomas Gainsborough thought of these people?

3 A Farmer's Tasks

B Ploughing with oxen

If you have ever lived near or stayed on a farm, you may have noticed the many different jobs farmers have to do each month. In the eighteenth century, running a farm meant a lot of hard work as there were few machines around to take the sweat out of day-to-day tasks.

How would you like this as a job? Mary Rendall was your age and worked full time on a farm:

❛ I got up early as half-past two, three, four or five, to get cows in, feed them, milk them, and look after the pigs. I then had breakfast, and afterwards went into the fields. I used to drive the plough, pick stones, weed, pull turnips, when snow was lying about, sow corn, dig potatoes, hoe turnips and reap. I did everything that boys did. Master made me do everything. I took a pride to it, when I used to reap, to keep up with the men. ❜ (A)

One of the most important tasks was ploughing. Farmers used their ploughs to turn over the soil to make the land ready for planting seed. In 1700, the plough consisted of a *coulter* (a blade which cut the soil), a *share* (a blade which cut the soil in a different direction) and a *mould board* (an iron or wooden plate which came behind the share and turned over the piece of soil cut by the two blades). **B** shows a man ploughing. The plough was usually pulled along by oxen.

Ploughing was normally carried out in the autumn and winter months. After the strips had been ploughed, the next stage was to break up the soil even more, to get it ready for sowing. A harrow was used for this purpose. The first harrows were made of hawthorn bushes dragged over the ground with heavy weights on top of them. By the eighteenth century, the harrow consisted of a wooden frame of bars and cross-bars with wooden pegs sticking downwards. These were designed to produce a fine *tilth* (seed bed). Later harrows had iron teeth.

Having prepared the soil, farmers would then sow seed by hand. This was usually done in the spring. Sowing seed by hand is known as *broadcasting* and was not as wasteful as it sounds. The sower would take even paces and cast the oats and barley seed to one side or another with great care. An experienced sower could sow seed with both hands, throwing the seed to right and left as he went along. It took years to perfect this skill. **C** shows a sower in action.

Once the crop had started to grow, the farmer removed any weeds which might stifle the growth of the oats or barley. Most farm land was weeded by using a hand-hoe or a weeding hook.

Harvesting took place in August. The corn was cut with a sickle with an edge like a saw. Hay-making was carried out using a scythe. After the crops had been gathered in, the grain was threshed in a barn using a flail. In this way the ears of corn were separated from the *chaff* (straw).

For a farmer's tasks in October, we can look at a farming magazine issued in October, 1726:

❛ October: If the roads are still good, make an end of bringing home such things as may be wanting on your farm in the winter and when your teams go to market, bring home such manures as you can get.
Also lay straw, that it may rot and serve to help the stiff lands.
This is a good month for brewing, the air being warm

enough for the fermenting of drink . . .

Now take up your carrots, sown in the spring, and after having cut off their tops close to the root, let them dry three or four days and lay them up in dry sand, or dry leaves of trees till you carry them to market.

Your potatoes are now very good and fit for market. Have regard to the fences of your wheat field, for while the wheat is tender, cattle should not come upon it.

Carry on making cider and gather your winter-fruits for keeping in dry weather, taking care that your fruiteries have air and that no bruised fruits are laid up with the rest.

You may plant trees in your hedgerows if the ground is light and dry.

You may bring in stocks of bees but do not buy from too many places in case your apiary is disturbed by wars. Collect still acorns for your hogs and keep them still in the woods.

Now begin to kill swine for bacon and pickled pork. Dry your beef, for now fires are kept: the season is warm enough for the flesh to take salt. **)** **(D)**

E shows the front page of an early book on farming showing some of a farmer's tasks.

C Sowing seed by hand

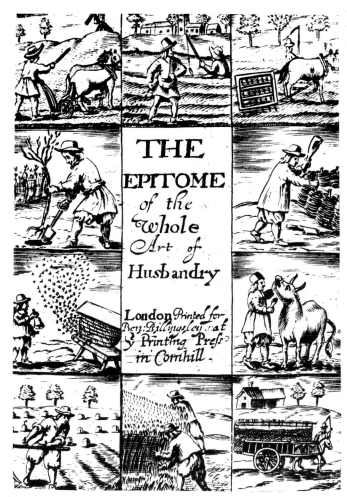

E A farmer's tasks, from *The Epitome of the Whole Art of Husbandry* 1689

??????????????????

1 Make a table to show the farm tools you have learned about, their uses and the season when used. You should include: plough, harrow, hand-hoe, sickle, scythe. Set your table out like this:

Farm tool	Season	Uses

2 You can see farm labourers sowing seed broadcast in **C** and **E**.
  a What differences can you see between these two pictures?
  b How do you account for these differences?

3 Using the text, the evidence and the previous chapters, write about the advantages and disadvantages of open-field farming methods (1700-1750): Why do you think changes in farming took place very slowly during this period?

4 The Improvers: Jethro Tull

Jethro Tull (1674-1741) was one of the first of a number of men who helped to bring about changes in farming methods. His ideas and inventions were to alter the way in which crops were sown and looked after. He had been a lawyer in his early life but had taken up farming because he had suffered from poor health. When he began working on his father's farm at Mount Prosperous in Berkshire, it struck him that certain ways of farming were very wasteful. He was especially worried about the amount of seed wasted by the normal method of broadcasting seed (see chapter 3). He told his farm workers to try planting seeds in rows. These could be hoed more easily while the crop was growing. Some labourers objected to this. They said that seed ought to be sown according to the old traditions and as laid down in the Bible.

Despite this, Tull carried on trying to find a better way of sowing seed. Looking at a church organ one day gave him a brainwave:

❝ *At last, I pitched upon a groove, tongue and spring in the soundboard of the organ. With these a little altered and some parts of two other instruments added to them, I made my machine.* ❞ (A)

He called the machine a 'drill' because when farmers used to sow their peas and beans in channels or furrows, they used to talk about 'drilling' them. B is a modern painting, showing the drill in use.

The seed-drill sowed the seeds and covered them up in one operation. It scratched a shallow channel in the soil, dropped the grains along it at regular intervals and then filled up the channel with soil again. The drill had two large wheels at the front, two small wheels at the back and was pulled along by a horse. Tull claimed that anyone using his drill would obtain a seven- or eight-fold increase in his corn harvest. At first there were a lot of technical problems with this machine and things often went wrong.

Between 1711 and 1714, Tull travelled across the Continent. He visited Holland, France and Germany. He visited French vineyards and watched workers hoeing between the rows of grapes. It seemed that hoeing let air get at the roots of plants and cleared away weeds. Crop yields were heavier because plants did not have to fight for their share of sunlight and water.

From 1714 onwards, Tull divided his land into long, narrow plots, each two metres wide with a space between

B Jethro Tull's seed-drill in action

C Tull's horse hoe

them. Women with hand-hoes cleared away any weeds between the plants. The next step was to fix a hoe onto a framework on wheels with the blade set just below the surface of the soil. The hoe could then be drawn up and down the field by a horse, uprooting the weeds and dropping them off as it went. **C** is a drawing of Tull's horse hoe.

In 1733, Tull published a book about it called *The New Horse Hoeing Husbandry*. He was upset to find that many of his ideas were mocked:

❝ A wheat-field sown according to the principles laid down by Mr. Tull must present a very odd appearance, since he sows only two to four rows of seeds, each seven to twelve inches apart, to a 'ridge' of soil; there are intervals of two and a half to five feet between each of these 'ridges'. Mr. Tull also asserts that with adequate tillage (ploughing and hoeing), yet without manures, it is possible to repeat the same crop on the same portion of soil from one year to the next. ❞ (D)

Tull was against the practice of manuring land because he thought that manure contained the seeds of weeds. He believed that hoeing was enough to keep the soil fertile and that it was not necessary to feed the land with nutrients as well.

At the time of Tull's death in 1741, his ideas had had little effect on farming. However by 1782 James Caird, an agriculturalist and writer, had improved the seed-drill a great deal. Farmers could now use it without fear of it breaking down. By the middle of the nineteenth century, most farmers used seed drills to sow their wheat. This is what an historian thinks of Tull's importance:

❝ Tull was a strange person. Some of his activities would not meet with the approval of modern farmers; he claimed, for example, that he had grown thirteen successive crops on the same ground without manure. Tull's reputation has been exaggerated. Yet he was important for his inventions — and also for the example

he set of studying things carefully and noting them down. Farmers were slow to take up his ideas and he was often regarded as a crank. But he was the forerunner of other developments in agricultural implements. ❞ (E)

??????????????????

1 Look carefully at **B**. Try to match up the numbers **1 – 5** with the words below. Two are done for you:
hoppers; funnels; sheats; harrow (**4**); shafts (**5**)
Then complete the following, using *some* of the words above:
Seed fell into the seedboxes fitted underneath the _____ . Then the seed fell into the _____ . These discharged the seed into the trunks at the back of the _____ . The iron share at the bottom of the _____ formed the furrow into which the seed fell.

2 **C** shows Tull's horse hoe.
a What other farming implement does the horse hoe look like?
b Can you think of *two* problems you might face when using the horse hoe?

3 Write a newspaper advertisement for Tull's drill. You should mention:
a how it works;
b its advantages;
c its appearance;
d its importance.

4 Imagine you were the historian who wrote **E**. What might you have said about Tull's
a early life?
b visits abroad?
c inventions?
d critics?

5 The Improvers: Townshend and Coke

A Viscount 'Turnip' Townshend (1674-1738)

B How the Norfolk four-course rotation worked

Year 1	The farmer grew turnips in long rows which could be kept hoed until the leaves were large enough to smother weeds. In this way the soil was given a fine tilth (texture). The stumps of the turnips were grazed off by sheep. Their dung enriched the soil.
Year 2	A crop of barley or oats was grown on the land which was then in very good condition, having plenty of nitrogen in it and being free from thistles, docks and dandelions.
Year 3	Clover or rye-grass was sown which replaced the nitrogen in the soil. At the end of the year, the pasture was cut for hay, grazed and thus manured.
Year 4	The land was in exactly the right condition for wheat which was sown in the autumn. In Year 5, the rotation would begin all over again with turnips.

Charles Townshend

Charles Townshend (**A**), nicknamed Turnip Townshend, retired from politics in 1730 and returned to his estates at Raynham, near King's Lynn in Norfolk. He found that the soil on his farms was in poor condition. It was badly drained and covered in coarse grass. However, just below the topsoil was *marl*, a sort of chalky clay rich in minerals. If dug up and mixed with topsoil, it gave the soil extra 'body'. So Townshend encouraged his tenant farmers to use marl to improve the quality of their soil. He also saw to it that on heavy, marshy land, drainage ditches were dug to prevent crops from becoming waterlogged.

As Townshend had once worked in Holland as a diplomat, he knew a lot about the progress in farming made by Dutch farmers. A system of crop rotation had been in use there since the mid-seventeenth century and Townshend worked hard to make the system well known. **B** shows how a 'Norfolk' four-course rotation worked.

This rotation meant that a third of the arable land was no longer left empty. Cattle and sheep did not have to be killed off in large numbers every winter as turnips and hay could be used to keep them alive. Stronger farm animals could be reared and fresh meat and milk could be sent to people in towns, even in winter.

Townshend also used Tull's machines (see chapter 4) for drilling and hoeing and had his estates enclosed (divided up into 'patchwork' fields surrounded by hedges or fences). He built a turnpike road to help farmers. Finally, he gave his tenant farmers long leases so that they could carry out the new rotations and improvements without the fear of being turned off their land.

In 1771, thirty-three years after Townshend's death,

D Thomas Coke inspecting his flock of Southdown sheep at Holkham

E Methods used by Coke to improve his land

Improvement	Result
Marling	Sandy soil able to hold more moisture and nutrients
Four-course rotation	More cattle fodder in winter
Introduction of special grasses	Better quality hay and more of it
Stall feeding	Cattle could be kept in better condition
Rotherham plough	More efficient ploughing; horses used rather than oxen
Tull's seed drill	Less seed wasted; easier hoeing
Underground drainage	Fewer problems with flooding; less crop disease

Arthur Young, a writer (see chapter 6), visited Norfolk. He had this to say about Norfolk agriculture:

❛ The great improvements have been made by means of the following:

First, by enclosing without the assistance of Parliament.
Second, by the spirited use of marl and clay.
Third, by the introduction of an excellent course of crops.
Fourth, by the culture of turnips, well hand-hoed.
Fifth, by the culture of clover and ray-grass.
Sixth, by landlords granting long leases.
Seventh, by the county being divided into large farms.

Take any one from the seven, and the improvement of Norfolk would never have existed. ❜ (C)

Thomas Coke

Thomas Coke (1754-1842) was another of the men who spread new ideas about farming. From 1776 he owned land at Holkham, Norfolk, close to Charles Townshend's estates. So many changes had taken place in Norfolk since the seventeenth century that all Coke had to do was to carry on with the work started by other members of his family. He did so with great success. **D** shows Coke inspecting his flock of Southdowns. **E** shows how Coke improved his land.

A large part of the Holkham estate was rented out to tenant farmers. This brought in £12 000 a year. Coke educated his tenant farmers in the new ways of farming and gave them long leases on their farms. By 1816 the value of the rents had doubled.

In 1778 Coke decided to hold a sheep-shearing festival at Holkham. Soon the festivals, which lasted four days, were being held every year. Up to 7000 people from all over Britain and even from the Continent attended the

F A sheep-shearing festival at Woburn

shows. Cattle, pigs, sheep and horses were on display. Early types of farm machinery could be seen and ploughing competitions were held. People went away from Holkham impressed by the friendly atmosphere and full of plans to copy Coke's ideas. The last sheep-shearing was held in 1821 but County Shows and Agricultural Fairs still go on in many parts of Britain today.

??????????????????

1 Copy out the following chart, completing the information that is missing. The chart shows a four-course rotation.

	Field A	Field B	Field C	Field D
1730	Wheat	Turnips	Barley	Clover
1731	Turnips	Barley	?	?
1732	?	?	?	?
1733	?	?	?	?

How might the fields have been farmed under the old system?
Why is the new system better?

2 C tells us about a list of improvements Arthur Young noted after a visit to Norfolk. Rewrite the list in what you consider to be the order of importance of the improvements.
Give reasons why you think the first, second and third improvements were so important.

3 F shows a sheep-shearing festival at the home of the Duke of Bedford. Use the picture and the text to write an eye-witness account of what it might have been like to have attended a show like this at Holkham and what the show was *for*.

6 The Improvers: Bakewell and Young

Robert Bakewell

A and B were written and drawn around 1750. This long-legged, goat-like creature was reared mainly for its wool. Its milk was used for cheese-making and its dung manured land for wheat or barley. This animal was all skin, muscle and bone.

6 *His frame was large and loose, his legs were long and thick, his chin as well as his rump as sharp as a hatchet, his skin rattling on his ribs like a skeleton covered in parchment.* **9 (A)**

From 1750 onwards, the growth of towns led to a big demand for meat. Many farmers wanted to turn animals like their sheep into good meat producing animals. The spread of the four-course rotation (see chapter 5) meant that sheep and cattle could be fattened up on turnips or hay during the winter. Landowners began to choose their best animals and breed them to produce strong, healthy flocks. This is called 'selective breeding'. The man most famous for selective breeding in the late eighteenth century was Robert Bakewell.

Before the eighteenth century, sheep had been bred by the method known as 'cross-breeding' or 'out-breeding'. This meant mating animals of different breeds and hoping that their young would combine the best points of both breeds. Bakewell took two breeds of sheep, the old Leicester (used for mutton) and the Lincoln (a sheep bred for its wool), and successfully crossed them. He then managed to 'in-breed' a new sheep. This meant that he mated sheep from the same family. The new breed, the New Leicester, had a long fleece and produced a lot of

B Early sheep were long-legged, goat-like creatures

THE LEICESTERSHIRE IMPROVED BREED.

To thefe various and numerous tribes of this ufeful animal, we muft add, that, by the perfevering induftry and attention of Mr Bakewell, of Difhley, in Leicefterfhire, our breed of Sheep has been greatly improved; and he has been followed by many eminent breeders with nearly equal fuccefs.

It feems to be generally agreed, that in Sheep, as well as in all other animals, there is a certain fymmetry or

C The Leicestershire Improved Breed, a product of Bakewell's selective breeding system

rather fatty mutton. Later, other breeds of sheep were raised from the New Leicester (**C**).

Bakewell also tried to improve the English cow, the Longhorn. As the best beef comes from the rear end of a cow, he tried to breed an animal with larger rear parts. But Bakewell's new cow gave much less milk than the old Longhorn, and the larger rear gave beef that was too fat. However, he was more successful in his breeding of the modern shire horse which was used to plough fields instead of oxen.

People came from all over Britain and Europe to see Bakewell's horses, sheep and cattle. He was always willing to show people over his farm and give advice. The cleanliness of his stalls and sheds and his kindness to his animals impressed visitors. He opened a museum which housed skeletons of his prize animals and pickled joints of beef and mutton. Although none of his breeds survive, Bakewell's approach to selective breeding remains in use today. **D** shows how much Bakewell and other stock breeders achieved during the eighteenth century.

D Average weight of animals sold at Smithfield Market

	1700	1800
Black cattle	166.5 kg	360 kg
Sheep	13 kg	36 kg
Calves	22 kg	66 kg
Lambs	8 kg	22 kg

Arthur Young

The writer and journalist Arthur Young, who had once been a farmer, wrote about new farming methods so that people who could not travel to a model farm or a sheep shearing could learn about improved livestock and crops. **E** is from a report he wrote on the area of Cambo, Northumberland in 1769.

E

Rotations used on the Farms
1 Wheat, oats, oats, fallow
2 Barley, oats, oats, oats, fallow

Farm Animals
Oxen and horses: ploughs pulled either by two horses and two oxen or by three horses; a plough team could plough about 0.3 hectares a day; ploughing to a depth of 130 mm cost about 40p per hectare; a horse required 2 bushels of oats per week.

Food Prices
Bread 1p kilogramme   Butter 4.5p kilogramme
Meat 3p kilogramme   Milk 1p for 8 litres
Cheese 2p kilogramme

Arthur Young also had something important to say in 1770 about the spread of new farming ideas:

‘ *I would say that we owe the introduction of new ideas such as marling, turnips, carrots, clover, sainfoin* (hay), *water meadows, drilling, horse-hoeing, dibbling* (making holes in the ground for seeds) *to great farmers.* ’ (**F**)

By ‘great farmers’ Young meant men who owned from 500 to 2000 acres of land. As these men visited the estates of their friends, they noted down the farming changes they saw. They then tried out the new ideas on their own farms.

In 1784 Arthur Young began a farming magazine called *Annals of Agriculture.* One famous farmer who wrote articles for this magazine was King George III (1738-1820), nicknamed ‘Farmer George’. He wrote under the name of his farm manager, ‘Ralph Robinson’. George became so keen on farming that he turned part of Windsor Great Park into a farm. **G** shows the king sending the horse guards to market with vegetables from the royal farm.

G A cartoon drawn in 1786, showing King George III sending vegetables to market.

In 1793 the government set up a Board of Agriculture to help spread the new ideas. Sir John Sinclair, a Scottish landowner, became President of the Board and Arthur Young, Secretary. The board made a survey of farming methods throughout the country, and asked farmers to send in reports and articles. A survey was published for each county on its agriculture. The spread of the new agriculture was vital at this time because Britain was fighting a war against France (1793-1802, 1803-1815) and needed to grow more food. In 1821 the government closed down the Board of Agriculture.

??????????????????

1 a What were the three main uses of sheep before 1750?
b Why couldn't a farmer carry out selective breeding in an open-field village? (See chapter 1)
c Why do you think the New Leicester was said to produce 'coalheaver's mutton'?

2 Look at the statistics in **D** and draw them either as a graph or as a histogram. Then write a short paragraph to say why the animals increased in size so much.

3 In **E** Arthur wrote about crop rotations used in Cambo. Can you think of a reason why the use of these rotations was a mistake?

4 In **G** what can you see at points **1 – 4**? What does the artist want you to think about the king as an agricultural improver?

5 How did George III earn his nickname?

7 Enclosures: What, When and Why?

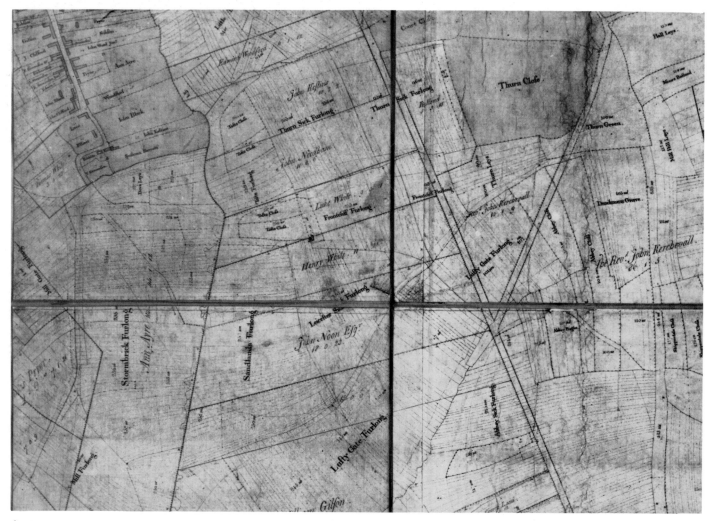

A Part of an old map, showing 'patchwork' fields and strips in Leicestershire

What were enclosures?

The word enclosure has two meanings: it is a hedge, wall or fence which a farmer puts around his land to stop animals from straying, and it can also mean the land which has been fenced or hedged off.

When the arable land around an open-field village was enclosed, all the strips were grouped together to form the 'patchwork' fields we know today. Land which had been used for grazing by the villagers (common land) was also enclosed, so that it could be used for growing crops. **A** is an old map showing 'patchwork' fields and strips in part of Leicestershire in 1798. Why are both types of field shown?

When did they happen?

Enclosures had been taking place in Britain since the thirteenth century. During the sixteenth century, much land was enclosed to improve sheep farming. By the eighteenth century more and more villages were being enclosed (**B**).

B Number of Enclosure Acts 1760-1830

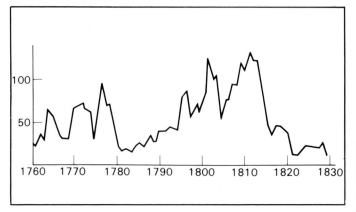

16

Why did they happen?

The main reason for making enclosures was money. On a large, compact farm with enclosed fields, a man could use the new farming methods to grow more wheat and raise more cattle. One writer, John Middleton, said this about enclosure in Middlesex:

❛ The benefits and advantages that would be gained from a general enclosure of commons are numerous. The opportunity it would afford of separating dry ground from wet, of well draining the latter, and liming the rotten parts, is of great consequence; as such an arrangement would, with the aid of intelligent breeders, be the means of raising a breed of sheep and neat cattle, far superior to the present race of wretched, half-starved animals now seen in such situations. It would have the effect of supporting more stock, upon the same quantity of food, by keeping the sheep and cattle within due bounds. Their restless and rambling disposition not only treads the grass off the ground, but also takes the flesh off their bones. It would tend to preserve improved breeds from that destructive malady, the rot, which makes such terrible havoc amongst our flocks. ❜ **(C)**

With healthier cattle and improved production, more money would be coming into the farm and this could be used for further improvements. The open-field farmers had used new farming methods with some success but it had been difficult for a farmer to grow new crops on his strips. Most of the strips in the open fields had to be sown and harvested at the same time. Enclosed fields gave farmers greater freedom to experiment with the 'new agriculture':

❛ There can be no question of the superior profit to the farmer by cultivating enclosures rather than open fields. In one case, he is in chains; he can make no variations according to the soil or prices or times. Whatever may be the advantages of varying the crops, he cannot change them – a mere horse in a team, he must jog along with the rest. ❜ **(D)**

Farmers could also make money by improving the soil. After the commons and wastes had been enclosed, they could be ploughed up and put under a four-course rotation. In Norfolk, the sandy soil produced little in its natural state but with marling and rotations it produced as much grain as any land in England.

The high price of grain gave a boost to enclosure. During the wars with France (1793-1815), huge sums of money were made from the sale of wheat. This money was often used to buy new machines and to drain land. It was important for the country to grow more food at this time because very little grain was being sent into Britain due to the war.

E Estimates of Population in England and Wales 1701-1801

Date	Millions	Date	Millions
1701	5.8	1761	6.5
1711	5.9	1771	7.0
1721	6.0	1781	7.5
1731	5.9	1791	8.2
1741	5.9	1801	9.1
1751	6.1		

A great increase in population in the eighteenth and nineteenth centuries meant that there were more people to feed than ever before. **E** shows how quickly the number of people in England and Wales increased between 1700 and 1800.

In early nineteenth-century Britain there were more people with more money to spend on food, living and working in growing industrial towns like Birmingham, Sheffield and Manchester. This created a demand for more food and a greater variety of food which led to more money being invested in farming and greater profits for farmers. Enclosure played some part in producing the wheat, meat and dairy produce needed to satisfy this demand. Open-field farming had produced enough food for a country made up of small villages but not enough for a growing industrial nation. One writer made the comment:

❛ The common field (open field) system was admirably suited to earlier times but is absurd today (1801) when millions of acres lie waste for want of a change of system, even though famine threatens at the gate. ❜ **(F)**

??????????????????

1 Look at **A**
a Who appears to have owned most land in this part of Leicestershire?
b Name the two women who owned land in this area.
c What sort of shape are most of the farms?
d After each name on the map, numbers are shown. What do you think these refer to?

2 Look at **B**
a In which decade did most enclosures take place? Why?
b During which decades did the number of enclosures decline?
c Is it true to say that between 1821 and 1830, there were less than half the number of enclosures which had taken place between 1761 and 1770?

8 Enclosures: Where and How?

Where did enclosures take place?

Map **A** shows where enclosures took place. You can see that they stretched from areas in the north, through the Midlands, and down to Sussex and Dorset on the south coast. Many parts of south-east England had been enclosed long before the eighteenth century.

How did enclosures take place?

B shows the two main ways in which enclosures were carried out. Up until 1740, most fields were enclosed by method 1, sometimes known as 'voluntary' enclosure because the villagers agreed to enclose land of their own free will. After 1750 method 2 was usually followed. A meeting of the freeholders had to be held to discuss plans for enclosure. When they had agreed on their plans, they would pass a resolution, or statement, which read something like this:

❝ *The commons and waste ground in the village in their present state are incapable of any considerable improvement, but if the same were divided and enclosed, it would*

A Where enclosures took place: shaded areas show percentages of common land enclosed by Act of Parliament

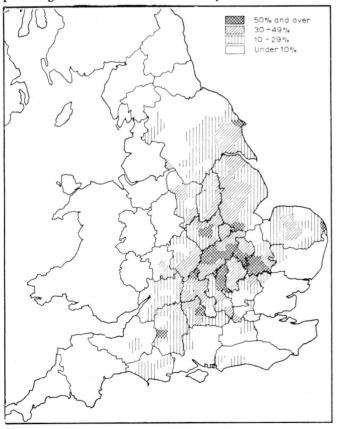

B How enclosures were carried out

Method 1	Method 2
All the people in the village who own land decide to enclose of their own free will	The owners of 80 per cent of the land decide to enclose the land around the village
A village meeting is held	They send a petition to Parliament
	Parliament passes an act for the village
The strips are enclosed	The strips are enclosed
'Patchwork' fields replace the old system of strip farming	

be of great advantage to the owners of land. In order to effect such division and enclosure, application shall be made to Parliament to divide and enclose the common fields, commons and wastelands around the village. ❞ (**C**)

A notice was fixed to the church door telling the rest of the villagers what had been decided upon at the meeting. Anyone who objected had to make their complaints known to the freeholders within three weeks. An application was then made to Parliament asking for an Act to be passed which would allow the open fields, commons and wastes to be enclosed.

Parliament would ask a few MPs, usually from the county in which the village to be enclosed lay, to form a committee which would look at the plan. They discussed it in detail, listened to any objections and made any changes they thought necessary. They had the right to recommend that the plan be thrown out but they usually gave it their approval. Parliament would then pass an Act ordering the village to be enclosed.

Under the Act, a group of responsible local people were appointed as 'commissioners' to make sure that the enclosures were fair to everybody. There could be any number of commissioners up to twelve but usually there were three. After 1790, there was only one commissioner appointed for each Act to try to keep the costs of enclosure down. The commissioners were landowners, lawyers, magistrates, clergymen or respected tradesmen. Each commissioner had to take an oath:

E Surveyors at work in the village of Henlow, Bedfordshire

❛ *I do swear that I will fairly and honestly according to the best of my skill and judgment, carry out the several powers and trusts reposed in me as a commissioner by virtue of an Act of Parliament, for dividing, and enclosing the lands, grounds and commons, without favour or affection or bad feeling to any person at all.* ❜ **(D)**

The commissioners next appointed surveyors and clerks, went to the village to be enclosed and tried to sort out who owned what land. The village people put in claims according to how much land they believed they owned and the commissioners tried to settle arguments over who owned the land and to share it out fairly. Meanwhile, the surveyors were busy measuring up the plots in the open fields and drawing up maps. **E** shows them at work. They had to redraw the map of the village, marking in the new enclosed fields and who owned them, the new roads, footpaths, tracks and drains. When the commissioners had finished their work, they signed and handed over the map which was stored in the church.

Unfortunately, enclosure cost a lot of money. The commissioners were well paid for their work and the cost of new roads, ditches, hedges and fences had to be met. **F** gives us an idea of what the charges were for 3000 acres of the Fitzwilliam Estates in Northamptonshire.

❛ *Cost of Enclosure of 3000 acres*
Parliamentary and legal expenses: £8000
Fences and hedges: £12 000
New farm buildings and roads: £4000 ❜ **(F)**

This was a time when a farm labourer earned about 50p a week. Certain farmers could not meet these costs and had to sell some of their land. To make things easier, Parliament passed a General Enclosure Act in 1801 which made it cheaper and simpler to enclose a village. By 1825, most of the open-field farm land had been enclosed in this way.

??????????????????

1 Look carefully at **E**
   a What sort of work are the surveyors doing?
   b Are they working in open fields or enclosed fields?
   c What is the job of the man on the far left of the picture?
   d What might he be saying to the surveyors?
   e Why was land surveyed?

2 Imagine you are a wealthy landowner in 1801 and you want to enclose your land. The other farmers in your village are not keen on the idea of enclosure.
   a Use the text and the evidence in chapters 7 and 8 to find *five* arguments you could use in favour of enclosure.
   b What counter-arguments might the farmers use against you?

9 Enclosures: The Results

A   How enclosure affected farming

New method or development	Result
More land cultivated	New crop rotations Greater quantity and variety of food, e.g. potatoes, turnips, swedes More fodder for animals More milk and dairy produce Fresh meat all the year round
Fences and hedges around fields	Selective breeding Fewer diseases amongst animals
Large farms and great estates	More jobs, bigger profits New farm buildings More machinery used Better drainage
New roads	Easier transport for men, food and animals.

A shows some of the changes which came about as a result of enclosure. Enclosure had its bad effects too. Although some freeholders and smallholders were better off, others lost the few strips they had farmed under the old system. Sometimes they also lost their cottages, where they had done some spinning and weaving. Some squatters were driven off the common land. **B** shows how the village of Stathern in Leicestershire changed in 1795 as a result of enclosures.

By 1800 a war was being fought with France and prices were high, which led to many anti-enclosure riots amongst the poor. Arthur Young believed that enclosure was to blame for their poverty. In 1801 he wrote:

❛ I don't want to argue about their good intentions; poor people look at facts, not intentions; and the fact is, by nineteen enclosure bills in twenty the poor are injured, in some cases grossly injured. It is said that the commissioners are sworn to do justice. What is that to the poor people who are left to suffer? What is it to the poor man to be told that the Houses of Parliament are very concerned about his property, while the father of the family is forced to sell his cow and his land because he can't own one without the other; and being deprived of his incentive to work, spends his money, gets into bad habits, enlists for a soldier and leaves his wife and children to the parish? The poor in these parishes may say and with truth, Parliament may be tender of property; all I know is, I had a cow, and an Act of Parliament has taken it from me.

Go to a pub in an area which has been enclosed and there you will see the cause of poverty. You will hear people say: 'Why should we stay sober? Why should we bother to save money? If we work hard, will we be able to buy a cottage? Will we be able to have a patch of land for a cow? Will we be able to plant out an acre of potatoes? All we can look forward to is the parish poorhouse. ❜ (C)

Historians and writers have argued about the results of enclosures for many years. The effect enclosures had on the poor is a matter of historical *controversy* because there is so much disagreement over what really happened. It

B   Changes in the village of Stathern as a result of enclosure

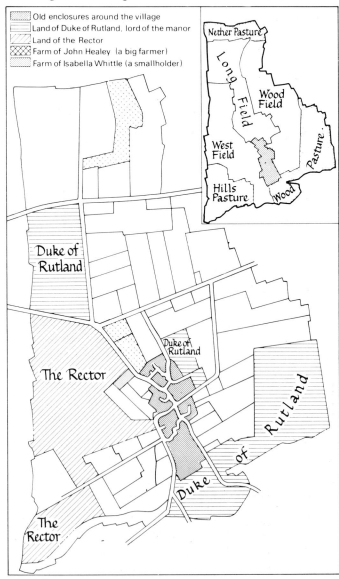

depends upon how you interpret the facts available. One historian, R. B. Jones, disagreed with Arthur Young. In 1977 he wrote:

It was once thought that enclosure meant the end of the small farmer. But detailed study has shown that their number went down in the early eighteenth century and actually rose during the main period of enclosure. Enclosure did not create a massive army of rural poor compelled to flock to towns in search of work. Many writers condemned enclosures on these grounds. There may have been cases of exploitation and dispossession but only where beef was profitable did the arable acreage shrink and the number of jobs decline. Otherwise enclosure increased the jobs. In 1802 there were 697 353 families engaged in farming; in 1831, at a time when the new towns were growing, this had increased to 761 348. (D)

???????????????????

1 Study the 'before and after' map, **B**. Describe how the size and shape of the land around the village have changed.

2 Historians divide historical evidence like **C** and **D** into two main groups – primary and secondary sources. **C** is an example of a primary source and **D** a secondary source. Look at the pieces of evidence again, then try to explain in your own words the main differences between a primary and a secondary source.

3 Do you think that the overall effects of enclosures were good or bad? Give reasons for your answer.

ENCLOSURE IN STATHERN

If you had been a villager in Stathern in 1792 (see opposite), what effect might the enclosures have had on your life? To find out, follow these directions:

1 Write out the alphabet. Below A put the number 1, below B write 2, and so on until you get to Z, 26.

2 Now write down your name. Below each letter of your name, write the appropriate number, e.g.

S U E   E V A N S
19 21 5   5 22 1 14 19

3 Look at the first two numbers (19 and 21 in the example above).
If the second number is greater than the first number, you have *gained* land as a result of enclosure.
If the second number is smaller than the first number, you have *lost* land as a result of enclosure.

4 If you have gained land, follow the instructions in the left-hand column. If you have lost land, follow the instructions in the right-hand column. Make a note of what happens to you at each stage.

GAINED	LOST
If the next letter in your name has an odd number below it, write down **O**; if even, write **E**.	If the next letter in your name has an odd number below it, write down **O**; if even, write **E**.
O: you gained land because you knew two of the commissioners well	**O**: you lost land because you couldn't prove ownership
E: you gained land because you bought out a poor farmer	**E**: you lost land because you couldn't afford the high cost of enclosure
Now look at the next letter.	Now look at the next letter
O: you decide to sell off some fields at a great profit	**O**: you decide to seek work on one of the new large farms
E: you decide to use new crop rotations and employ more men	**E**: you decide to buy another plot of land and and grow vegetables
Go to the next letter	Go to the next letter
O: you have borrowed too much money and go bust	**O**: you lose everything and go to Leicester to seek work
E: you make large profits and become rich	**E**: you do well and buy back some of your original land

Read through what happened to you. How would you have felt about enclosure if you had lived in Stathern? Things like this happened to real people in villages all over England as a result of enclosures.

10 The Farm Labourer and the Rural Poor

A A farm labourer setting off to work

C How a typical labourer lived

	s.	d.
Flour: 7½ gallons at 10d per gallon	6	3
Yeast (to make flour into bread)		2½
Salt		1½
Bacon: 1lb boiled with greens; the pot liquor with bread and potatoes makes a mess (stew) for the children		8
Tea: 1 oz		2
Sugar: ¼ lb		6
Butter (or lard): ½ lb		4
Soap: ¼ lb at 9d per lb		2¼
Candles: 1/3 lb at 9d per lb		3
Thread: for mending clothes		3
Total	8	11¼
Weekly earnings	8	6

The Farm Labourer

A shows a farm labourer in 1795. Such labourers had worked on the land for over a thousand years. The enclosures of the late eighteenth century (see chapters 7-9) helped to create more jobs for farm labourers. The new agriculture required more men for drilling, hoeing and looking after animals. With more wheat being planted out, more harvest hands were needed. In winter, labourers had to be employed for threshing and winnowing (separating grain from chaff). They were also needed for milling flour, malting barley, drying hops and making cheese. Often these labourers lived in very bad conditions.

In 1797, Sir Frederick Eden made a study of the labouring people. He told the story of a labourer's wife, Anne Strudwick:

❛Anne Hurst was born at Witley in Surrey; there she lived for the whole of a long life; and there she died. As soon as she was thought able to work, she went into service. Before she was twenty she married James Strudwick who, like her own father, was a day labourer. With this husband she led a contented, hard-working life, somewhat more than 50 years. He worked more than 60 years on one farm; and his wages, summer and winter were regularly one shilling a day. He never asked more, nor was offered less. They had between them seven children. Strudwick continued to work till within seven weeks of the day of his death; and at the age of 80 in 1787, he died.

Anne Strudwick survived her husband about seven years. Though bent with age and illness, she was too proud to ask for help from the parish and she got a job weeding a gentleman's garden. ❜ (**B**)

During her lifetime, Anne Strudwick may have found it hard to make ends meet. **C** shows a typical labourer's weekly budget in 1795.

Labourers like James and Anne Strudwick lived close to poverty for most for their lives. These people were the backbone of the agricultural revolution. Without them, the great changes could not have taken place.

The Rural Poor

In the late eighteenth and early nineteenth centuries poverty was a major problem. The rapid increase in population meant that during times of depression in

D Attempts by the Government to solve the problem of the poor

Date	Act	Importance
1597	Poor Law	Each parish had to look after its own poor. The money for this was raised by making the better-off people pay a tax (the poor rate). The money was used to buy clothes, food, fuel for the poor.
1722	Workhouse Act	Parishes were allowed to set up 'workhouses' or 'poor-houses'. Poor people had to enter the poor-house to get food, shelter and clothing.
1782	Gilbert's Act	Parishes were given the power to help each other deal with the problem of the poor. 'Able-bodied' (healthy) people could be given help *outside* the poorhouse.

farming and industry there were many more poor people to look after.

The problem of what to do with poor people had existed for centuries. **D** shows how Parliament attempted to deal with the problem.

E shows a workhouse in 1720. The paupers were often set simple tasks to help pay for the cost of running the workhouse. In 1783, a poet, George Crabbe, described a workhouse:

‘ *This is the house which holds the parish poor,*
Whose walls of mud scarce bear the broken door;
Here where the stinking vapours play,
And the dull wheel hums doleful through the day.
Here are the children who know no parents' care;
Parents who know no children's love live there!
Heart-broken old ladies on their joyless beds,
Abandoned wives and mothers never wed.
Downcast widows, with unheeded tears
And crippled age, with more than childhood fears.
The lame, the blind, and far the happiest they,
The moping idiot and the madman gay.
Here too, the sick, their final doom receive,
Here brought amid the scenes of grief to
grieve. . . . . ’ (**F**)

The Poor Law worked well while the population did not increase much and while prices were low, but it broke down in the late eighteenth century when rising prices, unemployment and an increase in the population made it impossible for parishes to cope. A new system of poor relief had to be found.

Providing for and employing all the Poor in Gr. Britain

The Poor when manag'd, and employ'd in Trade , —
Are to the publick Welfare, usefull made ; ·
But if kept Idle from their Vices Spring
Whores for the Stews, and Soldiers for the King .

E Life in the workhouse, as shown on an eighteenth-century playing card

??????????????????

1 Tell the story of the Strudwick family. Describe: **a** their home; **b** their clothes; **c** their food.

2 Which *two* pieces of evidence **A – C** best illustrate the life-style of a typical farm labourer and his family? Give reasons for your answer.

3 a Explain the meaning of these words: *pauper, poor rate, poor-house.*
b Where did poor people go to obtain money, food and shelter in 1780?
c Where do they go today to get these things?
d According to **F**, there were *six* different types of poor person housed in the poor-house. Make a list of the different types of poor people there. Can you think of any types of poor person the writer has left out?
e In **E**, what can you see at points **1 – 5**?

11 The Speenhamland System

A Inside a poor labourer's cottage

Picture the scene. It is 6 May 1795 and a group of justices (magistrates) are meeting at the Pelican Inn, Speenhamland, to discuss what is to be done about poverty in this part of Berkshire.

A shows the kind of conditions in which many poor labourers were living.

B shows why poor people were going hungry. Since 1775 the price of bread in England had been increasing.

To make matters worse, Britain had entered into a war with France in 1793. This led to shortages of certain items and after 1795 prices went up even higher. Wages did not rise at the same rate and many workers could not make ends meet. Labourers were forced to seek help from the parish and in the spring of 1795 there were food riots in various parts of the country.

The old system of Poor Relief had meant that parishes had to look after their own poor by raising money (the poor rate) for them. By the 1790s, high unemployment and bad harvests led to a very high poor rate. Poor farmers could hardly afford to pay.

The justices at Speenhamland met to see if they could

B Average price of bread in London 1765-1800
(in pence per 4lb)

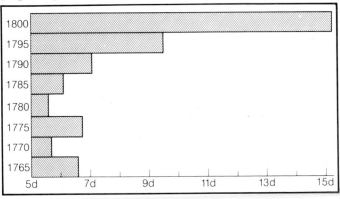

D The scale of allowances drawn up under the Speenhamland System

Income for:	When the gallon loaf costs:												
	1s 0d		1s 1d		1s 2d		1s 3d		1s 4d		1s 5d		1s 6d
Single man	3	0	3	3	3	6	3	9	4	0	4	0	4	3
Husband and wife	4	6	4	0	5	2	5	6	5	10	5	11	6	3
Husband, wife and one child	6	0	6	5	6	10	7	3	7	8	7	10	8	3
Husband, wife and two children	7	6	8	0	8	6	9	0	9	6	9	9	10	3

work out a different way of helping the poor. William Budd, Deputy Clerk, said that a new system of poor relief was needed. The parish could not cope with the number of people made poor by high prices and low wages. The magistrates finally agreed upon a new system of helping the poor. Not only would they give cash to those out of work, they would also make up the wages of those in work so that they could buy enough to eat. This 'Speenhamland System' was soon copied by parishes all over the south of England and affected the working of the Poor Law for nearly forty years. **C** is from the local paper, *The Reading Mercury*, a few days after the meeting:

❛ *At a general meeting of the justices on Wednesday 6th May at the Pelican Inn in Speenhamland, for the purpose of discussing wage levels, it was decided that the present state of the poor law requires further assistance.*

The justices recommend to the farmers and others in the county to increase the pay of their labourers in proportion to the present price of food.

When the loaf of flour weighing 8lb 11oz shall cost 1s (5p), then every poor and hardworking man shall have for his own support 3 shillings weekly, either produced by his own or his family's labour or an allowance from the poor rates: and for the support of his wife and every other member of his family 1/6d (7½p).

When the loaf shall cost 1s 4d (6½p), then every poor and hardworking man shall have 4 shillings (20p) weekly for his own and 10d (4p) for the support of every other person in his family. And as the price of bread rises or falls, 3d to the man and 1d to every other of his family on which 1d of the loaf rises above 1s (5p). ❜ (C)

D is a scale showing the income which the justices agreed that men and their families should receive, either as payment for their labour or as allowance from the poor rates.

In 1797 Sir Frederick Eden attacked this system:

❛ *In many parishes in Berkshire, relief from the Poor Rate is granted not only to the elderly and the sick but also to the healthy and hard-working men who had never asked the parish for assistance. There was no doubt that hard times required an increase in wages for farm labourers . . . . But there were surely other ways of making such an increase . . . .* ❜ (E)

F shows some of the results of the Speenhamland System.

F The results of the Speenhamland System

> 1 Many people were saved from starvation at a time of low wages and high prices.
> 2 Many labourers could see no point in working hard to obtain an increase in pay because when their wages went up, the parish would pay them less. Lazy people got as much money as hard workers.
> 3 The poor rates increased a great deal. This made some farmers poorer.
> 4 Wages were kept low by some farmers as they knew that the wages of their labourers would be made up to a certain amount by the parish.
> 5 Some historians have argued that the Speenhamland System may have led to larger families. Under the new system, a man received more money from the parish if he had a wife and children.

??????????????????

1 Put factors **a** to **d** into what you think the magistrates at Speenhamland considered their order of importance for introducing the system:
  a the price of bread;
  b the weekly wage earned by a farm labourer;
  c whether the farm labourer was married or not;
  d the number of children in the farm labourer's family.

2 Look at **A** to **F** carefully. What do you think was said by the other five justices in the Pelican Inn after William Budd had finished his speech?

3 In **E**, Sir Frederick Eden hints that there might have been more sensible ways of attacking the problem of poverty. Can you think of two other ways of helping the poor other than by making their wages up to a certain level?

12 The Corn Laws

If you turn back to the chart showing the farm labourer's weekly budget in chapter 10, you will see that in 1795 some families had very little variety in what they ate. Many people lived off a diet of bread and not much else. The Speenhamland System (see chapter 11) was based on the price of bread. Chart **A** shows how the price of bread varied according to whether wheat was plentiful or not.

You can see that when there is a surplus or glut of a crop like wheat, the price goes down; when there is a shortage, the price goes up. **B** shows the price of wheat per quarter between 1750 and 1860.

With the great increase in population of the early nineteenth century, the demand for bread increased. Open fields were enclosed (see chapters 7-9), new methods of farming were tried out and some common land was ploughed up. In this way, Britain was normally able to grow enough food to feed her people. When there was not enough, due to bad weather or crop disease, wheat could be brought into Britain from countries like France or Poland.

In 1793, the war with France meant that very little

A The link between wheat supplies and the price of bread

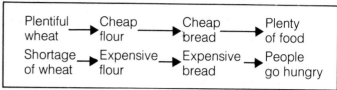

| Plentiful wheat | → | Cheap flour | → | Cheap bread | → | Plenty of food |
| Shortage of wheat | → | Expensive flour | → | Expensive bread | → | People go hungry |

B Price of wheat per quarter 1750-1860 (in shillings and pence)

1750	25s. 6d.	1790	50s. 0d.	1830	65s. 2d.
1760	24s. 8d.	1800	98s. 2d.	1840	65s. 10d.
1770	45s. 1d.	1810	96s. 0d.	1850	44s. 1d.
1780	39s. 10d.	1820	57s. 5d.	1860	43s. 11d.

wheat was brought into Britain from abroad. Prices went up and farmers were encouraged to grow more. Many landowners became very well off:

❛ You sometimes see a pianoforte in a farmer's parlour; a servant is sometimes found and a post-chaise to carry their daughters to assemblies, the milliner's or the dancing master's. These ladies are often educated at

E An Anti-Corn Law cartoon, drawn in 1815

boarding schools and the sons at the University to be made parsons . . . . .

Instead of walking, the farmers ride to market, even within short distances. Instead of going home to dinner, many of them dine at their clubs at the different inns. Many of those who do, remain after dinner to drink wine. Instead of country squires, we now have a breed of country gentleman farmers. **,** **(C)**

As the war went on, the price of wheat continued to rise until 1810 (see **B**). By 1815, the war was over. Many farmers became worried about wheat being imported into Britain again. Wealthy landowners thought they would be ruined. In February 1815, they persuaded Parliament to pass a *Corn Law* which stated that no foreign wheat would be allowed into Britain until the price at home reached 80 shillings a quarter.

Many ordinary people objected to this. Imports of

F Arguments for and against the Corn Laws

> ### Arguments in favour of the Corn Laws
> 1 British farmers would receive a reasonable price for their wheat.
> 2 Britain would not have to depend on other countries for her food.
> 3 Food prices would be kept stable.
> 4 Agriculture would improve as large sums of money made on selling corn could lead to more investment in farming.
> 5 They would encourage competition between different parts of the country to see which area could produce most corn and benefit from the high prices.
> 6 In the long run, it would lead to cheaper bread.
>
> ### Arguments against the Corn Laws
> 1 Factory owners said that if the price of bread was kept high, they would have to pay their workers higher wages. This would mean an increase in the amount charged for their goods. They would sell less and employ fewer people.
> 2 Poor people said that the Corn Laws would mean higher prices for food and make it more difficult for them to make ends meet.
> 3 It was claimed that the landowners were being given special favours at the expense of the rest of the population.
> 4 Small farmers would not benefit much and some would face ruin. The men who would benefit most would be the corn-dealers who bought up large stocks of corn, kept it, and sold it when the price was right.
> 5 There would be more unemployment (see point 1).
> 6 They would lead to a greater gap between the very rich and the very poor.

foreign grain meant cheap bread. Poor workers thought the Corn Law would push the price of bread up. Factory owners also opposed the Corn Law – can you guess why? There were riots and petitions against the Corn Law: 'No Corn Bill! No starvation! No landlords!' was the cry. A mob of people marched to the house of Frederick Robinson, the President of the Board of Trade. They thought he was responsible for bringing in the Corn Law:

' *As soon as they found his house, they broke the windows on every floor, bashed in the shutters and split the door into pieces. Rushing into the house, they cut to pieces many valuable pictures, destroyed the furniture and threw the rest into the street to be trampled into pieces.* **,** **(D)**

E is an anti-Corn Law cartoon.

The Corn Law did not always work well. When the harvest was very good, the price of wheat fell and to protect farmers from foreign competition, all grain was kept out. Above 80 shillings, huge amounts of grain could be shipped into Britain. In fact the price of corn rarely reached 80 shillings. So, in 1827, the government brought in a sliding scale. This meant that if wheat was plentiful and cheap, foreign corn would be taxed heavily when it was brought into Britain. If wheat was scarce and dear in Britain, very little tax would be charged. **F** shows the arguments which were used in favour of and against the Corn Laws.

???????????????????

1 It is February 1815. You are Frederick Robinson's private secretary. A mob of angry people has burst into his house. Robinson asks you to make a speech to the crowd designed to calm them down. In your speech you are to include as many arguments in favour of the Corn Laws as you can.
  a What would you actually say in your speech?
  b What counter-arguments do you think members of the crowd might use against you?

2 Look at **B** carefully. Draw a histogram to show the price of wheat 1750-1860. Then explain:
  a Why the price of wheat was higher in 1810 than in 1790.
  b Why the price of wheat went down between 1810 and 1820 (Clue: war).

3 Write short answers to the following:
  a When was the Corn Law passed by Parliament?
  b What did the Corn Law state?
  c Why was the Corn Law passed?
  d Outline the main arguments for and against the Corn Laws.

13 Captain Swing

What would you do if you were a farmer in the 1830s and you received a note like **A**?

Sir,
This is to let you know that if your threshing machines are not destroyed by you directly, we shall take action against them ourselves.
Signed on behalf of the whole,
Swing **(A)**

Ever since the end of the wars with France in 1815, there had been great hardship amongst farm labourers in Britain. Despite the passing of the Corn Laws (see chapter 12), the price of corn in some years had gone down. Some farmers had been ruined and many farm workers had lost their jobs. The winter of 1830 was particularly hard for farm labourers and their families. So in the south of England, the local justices had to make up the pay of labourers from the poor rate, in order to save them from starvation. In 1830, William Cobbett, a farmer and journalist wrote:

The wages for those who are employed on the land are, through all the counties that I have come, 7 shillings a week for married men and less for single men. A large part of them are not even at this season (spring) *employed on the land. In walking out yesterday, I saw three poor fellows digging stone for the roads, who told me they never had anything but bread to eat, and water to wash it down.* **(B)**

To make matters worse, many farmers in the south of England had started to use machines for threshing corn, (separating the ears of corn from the straw). The new machines did not result in many lost jobs but the labourers saw in them a symbol of their misery, so they started to set fire to hay-ricks and to destroy the threshing machines. **C** shows labourers burning hay-ricks on a farm in Kent in 1830. The labourers claimed that they were led by a man called Captain Swing, but no one can be certain whether he really existed. Those who took part in the 'Swing' riots were not trying to start a revolution. Their main aim was to persuade farmers to increase wages.

D shows where these disturbances took place.

In 1910 W. H. Hudson, a writer, wrote about a shepherd from Wiltshire called Caleb Bawcombe. Caleb could remember the riots of 1830 and what happened afterwards:

C Angry labourers burning the hay ricks on a farm in Kent

The farmers were very well off but they paid low wages to their miserable labourers. And if they were half-starved when there was work for all, what would their condition be when reaping machines and other new implements came into use? The men would not suffer it; they would gather together in bands everywhere and destroy the machinery; and so it came about that there were risings all over the land. **(E)**

Caleb Bawcombe worked for a farmer called Mr Ellerby who was quite well off and was keen to introduce new farming methods:

Mr Ellerby had been the first to introduce the new methods. He did not believe that the people would rise against him, for he well knew that he was regarded as a just and kind man and was even loved by his own labourers. But even if it had not been so, he would have carried out his resolution as he was a high-spirited man. One day, the villagers got together and came to his barns, where they set to work to destroy his new threshing machine. When he was told, he rushed out and went in hot haste to the scene. As he drew near, some person in the crowd threw a hammer at him, which struck him on the head and brought him senseless to the ground. **(F)**

Mr Ellerby was not badly injured. When he had recovered, the villagers had gone. None of Mr Ellerby's men was sure who had led the villagers or who had thrown the hammer. Later, the local justices found out that the hammer was the property of a shoemaker in the village. He was arrested and put on trial:

Tried with many others from other villages in the district at the Salisbury Assizes, he was found guilty and sentenced to transportation for life. Yet the Doveton shoemaker was known to everyone as a quiet, harmless young man and to the last he claimed that he was innocent, for though he had gone with the others to the farm, he had not taken the hammer and was guiltless of having thrown it. **(G)**

By 1831, nine men had been hanged for taking part in the 'Swing' Riots and 457 men and boys transported. One of the men hanged was 19. His offence? He had knocked the hat off a wealthy farmer's head. Hudson concluded:

It was necessary to strike terror into the people. . . after the business was done with, the farmers were still anxious and began to show it by holding meetings and discussions on the condition of the labourers. Everybody said that the labourers had been properly punished; but at the same time, it was admitted that they had some reason for their discontent. With bread so dear, it was hardly possible for a man with a family to support himself on seven shillings a week, and it was agreed to raise the wages by one shilling. But by and by, when the anxiety had died out, the farmers cut off the extra shilling and wages were what they had been.

But there were no more risings. **(H)**

D Areas of England where riots took place 1830-32

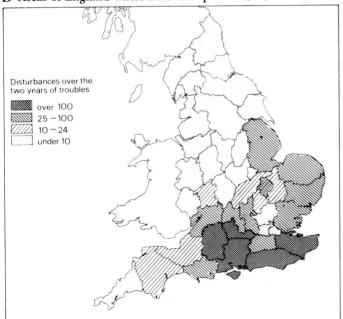

Disturbances over the two years of troubles

- over 100
- 25 – 100
- 10 – 24
- under 10

???????????????????

1 a How reliable is **C** as a piece of historical evidence?

b According to **E**, what was the *main* reason for labourers wishing to destroy the new farm machines?

2 a Draw three columns with the following headings:

Very serious disturbances (over 100 riots)	Serious disturbances (25 – 100 riots)	Quite serious disturbances (10 – 24 riots)

Using **D** and an atlas, put the counties below into their appropriate columns:

Wiltshire	Suffolk	Cambridgeshire
Berkshire	Essex	London
Dorset	Hampshire	Bedfordshire
Sussex	Surrey	Northamptonshire
Kent	Oxfordshire	Worcestershire
Lincoln	Gloucestershire	Devon
Norfolk	Huntingdonshire	Somerset

b Can you think of *three* reasons why disturbances took place in the counties in the 'Very serious' column? (Clues: wages, machinery, unemployment)

14 The Tolpuddle Martyrs

James Brine
Aged 25

Thomas Stanfield
Aged 51

John Stanfield
Aged 25

George Loveless
Aged 41

James Loveless
Aged 29

A Five of the 'Tolpuddle martyrs'

In 1834 six farm labourers from the Dorset village of Tolpuddle were transported to Australia for 'taking an illegal oath' at a meeting of a small trade union. **A** shows five of the six men involved.

The Swing riots of 1830 (see chapter 13) had left their mark on the small villages of Dorset. Landlords and JPs were afraid that riots might break out again. None of the six Tolpuddle labourers had been involved in the Swing riots, however. George Loveless, their leader, was widely respected for his honesty and good character.

❛ *He is a man of good natural intelligence, possessed of sound powers of concentration and application and moreover he has taught himself to read after his long hours of labour in the field . . . over the years he has built up a small library of religious books at great cost to himself. For several years he has been a lay preacher, an attainment that indicates his desire to reform and guide, if not lead his fellow beings.* ❜ **(B)**

Loveless wanted to start a trade union for farm workers to campaign against wage cuts and help its members in time of sickness and poverty. He arranged a meeting in Tolpuddle between farmers and labourers.

It was decided that the farmers would raise wages to match those earned by men in other districts. The farmers did not keep their word, however, so labourers had to accept a very low standard of living. William Cobbett wrote:

❛ *The dwellings of labourers are little better than pig-beds, and their looks indicate that their food is not nearly equal to that of a pig. Those wretched hovels are stuck upon little beds of ground on the roadside. In my whole* life I never saw human wretchedness equal to this: no, not even amongst the free negroes in America. ❜ **(C)**

In June 1833 someone suggested forming 'A Society of Agricultural Labourers' in Tolpuddle, a sort of trade union. **D** shows the development of Trade Unions up until 1834.

In trying to join the GNCTU, the Dorset labourers were acting in a way which the farmers thought was very dangerous. There were many unions in the north of England but few in the south. It looked as if the ideas of Robert Owen and John Doherty were spreading all over the country. The government and the justices were determined to stop this. An example had to be made of the men from Dorset.

George Loveless and his friends decided upon a secret ceremony for new members of their union. New members were blindfolded and led into a room. Their eyes were uncovered. On the wall was a painting of a skeleton over six feet high, holding a scythe. After they had stared at the skeleton for a few minutes, the new members had to kneel down and their eyes were rebandaged. They then kissed the Bible and swore a secret oath. Such ceremonies had been used by Friendly Societies and Trade Clubs for years, but under an act of 1797 it was illegal to give or take a secret oath.

❛ *Any person who shall become a member of such a society, or take an oath or agree to any test or declaration not authorized by law. . . . Any person who shall administer, or be present at, or who shall cause such oath to be administered, although not actually present at the time. . . WILL BECOME GUILTY OF FELONY (a serious crime) AND LIABLE TO BE TRANSPORTED FOR SEVEN YEARS.* **(E)**

George Loveless and his fellow labourers were arrested and put on trial at Dorchester. Loveless told the judge:

' My lord, if we have broken the law, it was not done

D The development of trade unions 1700-1834

Event/Development	Importance
1700-1799 Trade clubs and friendly societies	Clubs formed to protect interests of workers. Many clubs met in pubs. Benefits for members who were unemployed, sick or hard up.
1799-1800 The Combination Acts	Government worried by ideas coming out of revolutionary France. All combinations (unions) of workers and employers illegal. Acts difficult to enforce.
1824 Repeal of the Combination Acts	Mainly due to the campaigns of Francis Place, a tailor, and Joseph Hume MP.
1825 Some restrictions on trade unions relating to 'molesting' and obstructing during a strike	Due to the wave of strikes which followed repeal of Combination Acts. Trade unions still remained legal, however.
1830 The National Association for the Protection of Labour (NAPL)	Started by John Doherty. The first large union, it had 100 000 members by 1831 and its own newspaper.
1834 The Grand National Consolidated Trades Union (GNCTU)	The work of Robert Owen, a socialist and reformer. A large union for all workers in all trades, this union aimed at changing the nature of society rather than just providing benefits for workers. George Loveless wanted the Tolpuddle labourers to join up with this union.

intentionally. We have injured no man's character, reputation, person or property. We were uniting together to preserve ourselves, our wives and our children from utter degradation and starvation. We challenge any man or any number of men to prove we have acted or intended to act different from that statement. **(F)**

The labourers were found guilty and sentenced to seven years transportation. Before being transported to Australia, the labourers were sent to 'hulks' (prison ships) at Portsmouth. One of them wrote:

' Of all the shocking scenes I had beheld, this was the most distressing. There were confined in this floating dungeon nearly six hundred men, most of them double-ironed. You can imagine the horrible effects arising from the rattling of the chains, the filth and vermin produced by such a miserable crew, the oaths and shouts heard constantly among them. Nothing short of a descent into hell can be compared with it. **(G)**

There was an outcry after the men had been sentenced. Meetings and demonstrations were held and petitions were signed all over the country. 30 000 people attended a rally in London led by Robert Owen. A committee, based in London, managed to get the sentences reduced and the public gave money to bring the men back from Australia and to buy them small farms. However, by transporting the six labourers, the government had dealt farm workers a heavy blow. Many men were now afraid to form unions.

??????????????????

1 Give *two* reasons why George Loveless wanted to form a union for farm labourers.

2 Why did government want to make an example of the Dorset labourers in 1834?

3 A is from a copy of *Cleave's Penny Gazette*, published in May 1838.
   a What sort of person might have drawn these pictures?
   b What sort of people was the artist trying to make the labourers look like?
   c Why do you think the newspaper printed the ages of the men underneath each picture?

4 Two newspapers reported the trial of the Dorset labourers. One, the 'True Sun' contained an article attacking the sentences and the way in which the men had been treated. The other, 'The Morning Post' approved of the harsh sentences and was against trade unions. Write the editorials which might have appeared in both these papers.

15 The Anti-Corn Law League

A The membership card of the Anti-Corn Law League

In the 1830s, many working people formed organizations to try to persuade others that the Corn Laws were unfair. They did not get very far with their campaigns because the only people who could change the Corn Laws were Members of Parliament, and few MPs took any notice of them.

In October 1838, a group of merchants and mill-owners set up the Manchester Association for the Repeal of the Corn Laws. Two leaders of the association were John Bright, a Rochdale factory owner, and Richard Cobden who owned a cotton-printing works near Manchester. A meeting of all men opposed to the Corn Laws was held in London in February 1839. There were speakers from Liverpool, Manchester, Glasgow, Leeds and Birmingham. They hoped to persuade MPs to repeal the Corn Laws at once but Parliament ignored them.

The Manchester speakers decided to set up an Anti-Corn Law League which would campaign against the Corn Laws and try to get them repealed. To belong to the league, you had to pay a membership fee of 25p a year. **A** shows the membership card given to members of the league.

Soon meetings of the league were being held all over the country. Each branch was asked to petition (send a demand to) the government to repeal the Corn Laws, giving reasons why the laws should be scrapped. This petition was sent to Parliament by a group of workers in Sheffield in 1841:

Your petitioners believe that the existing Corn Laws, by preventing the free exchange of our goods for the production of other countries, has restricted their sale in many parts of Europe and America. Foreign governments have imposed heavy tariffs (customs duties) in retaliation: Your petitioners have been used to misery and starvation because there are not enough jobs and with lower wages it has been impossible for them to feed their families because of the high prices caused by these laws. These unjust Corn Laws, if continued, will finally lead to great prosperity in other countries at our expense. **(B)**

The Anti-Corn Law League was in a hurry to get the Corn Laws changed and the quickest way to persuade MPs to vote for repeal was to speak to them in Parliament. This meant getting men who were against the Corn Laws elected to the House of Commons. After many campaigns, a total of eight Anti-Corn Law MPs were elected, including Richard Cobden. He said:

We want Free Trade in corn, because we think it just. Whether it becomes dearer with Free Trade – or whether it is cheaper, it matters not, provided the people have it at its natural price: we do not believe that Free Trade in corn will injure the farmer. Neither do we believe that it will injure the farm-labourer. We think it will enlarge the market for his labour, and give him a chance to find jobs, not only on the soil but that there will be a general rise in wages from the increased demand for employment in the towns. We do not expect it will injure the landowner in terms of money but it will reduce his political power. We believe that Free Trade will increase the demand for labour of every kind, giving employment to all those youths who are so desirous of setting out in the world. **(C)**

The MPs still did little. In 1842 Peel, the Prime Minister, changed the sliding scale of duty on corn imports, making the duty lower. It became necessary to drum up more support outside Parliament. From December 1842, an Anti-Bread Tax leaflet was published every week. Lectures and protest meetings were planned. The new Penny Post was used to send a pamphlet to every voter in England:

At the next election, you will have to choose between a bread-taxer and a candidate who will untax the poor man's loaf. The choice involves an awful responsibility. Think carefully before you decide. Examine the evidence which is put in your hands. **(D)**

By 1845, Cobden, Bright and ten other MPs were making regular speeches in the House of Commons against the Corn Laws. Cobden felt sure that Prime Minister Robert Peel, leader of the Conservative party, could be persuaded to repeal the Corn Laws. Peel had secretly decided in favour of repeal. The problem was that the Conservatives strongly supported the Corn Laws.

Before Peel could work out what to do, a serious famine hit Ireland, due to a disease of the potato. In Ireland, the potato was a staple crop. Within a few months, people were starving. In 1846, W. E. Forster visited a village in County Mayo, Ireland:

F Starving children searching for potatoes during the Irish potato famine

Out of a population of 240, I found thirteen already dead from want. The survivors were like walking skeletons; the men stamped with the livid mark of hunger, the children crying with pain, the women in some of the cabins too weak to stand. When I was there before, I had seen cows at almost every cabin and there were sheep and pigs owned in the village. But now all the sheep had gone, all the cows, all the poultry killed, only one pig left. **(E)**

F shows some starving Irish children searching for sound potatoes.

The supporters of the Anti-Corn Law League began a campaign to 'open the ports' because it was clear that unless cheap wheat was sent to Ireland, thousands more would die. As MPs discussed the matter, many Irish peasants starved. Soon, one million were dead.

Peel was convinced that the Corn Laws would have to go. In 1846, with the help of opposition parties in Parliament, he passed an act repealing the Corn Laws. The Anti-Corn Law League had won the battle for free trade. But for many Irish people, repeal had come too late.

????????????????????

1 Which of the following arguments against the Corn Laws carried most weight in the 1840s? Put them in order of importance:

  a The Corn Laws were un-Christian.
  b The Corn Laws led to unemployment.
  c The Corn Laws led to high food prices.
  d The Corn Laws helped only the wealthy landowners.
  e The Corn Laws led to homelessness.
  f The Corn Laws made trade difficult.
Give reasons for your selections.

2 Using the notes below, the text and any other information you can find, write a short essay on the life and work of Richard Cobden.

> **Richard Cobden (1804-1865)**
> Born in Sussex, educated at a private boarding school in Yorkshire; started work in his uncle's warehouse in London at 18; in 1831 set up a calico business in Lancashire; 1833-1839 travelled to France, Germany, USA; 1838-1846 fought for the repeal of Corn Laws; a good organizer and leader; became MP for Stockport in 1841; became more interested in politics than business and after repeal he was ruined because he had spent so much money on campaign; after repeal, opposed Factory Acts and trade unions but supported the idea of state education.

16 The Golden Age of Farming (1)

A Factors leading to the Golden Age of Farming 1840-1870

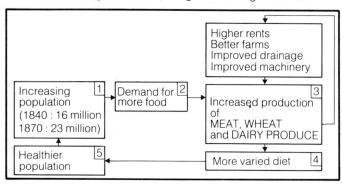

The years between 1840 and 1870 were very good ones for English farmers. **A** shows why.

Farmers made so much money during this period that it is known as 'the golden age of farming'. Many of them invested the profits they had made in new farm buildings, machinery and drainage schemes.

B shows a farm built for the Marquis of Bath at Longleat, Wiltshire, in 1859. Because it was so up to date and contained all the best equipment, it was known as a 'model farm'. The best known 'model farmer' in Britain

at this time was Prince Albert, the husband of Queen Victoria. He introduced a new type of farm called the Flemish farm. **C** is a picture of such a farm.

Built in 1858, the Flemish farm was made out of brick rather than wood. The stock-yard was in the centre with the stables on one side and an open yard on the other. Separated from the yard by a covered cart-way was the barn.

D shows how the farm was organized.

In the early nineteenth century, farm land had been badly drained by ridges and furrows. Now, improved drainage made the soil easier to work and meant that seed sown was less likely to rot. A special machine was invented for laying pipes, which cut the cost of drainage:

❛ *Twelve years ago (1839), draining tiles were made by hand and cost 50 shillings (£2.50) per 100. Pipes have been substituted for these, made by machinery, which squeezes out clay from a box exactly as macaroni is made in Italy. The cost of these pipes averages from 12 shillings to 20 shillings (60p to £1) per 1000. The new invention has made possible the drainage of land at a rate of £3 – £4 an acre.* ❜ **(E)**

B The Marquis of Bath's model farm at Longleat

In the 1850s, the government started to offer loans to farmers who wanted to drain their land. Millions of pipes were laid in Surrey, Berkshire and Bedfordshire but progress was slower in Durham and Yorkshire where heavy clay soils made pipe-laying difficult. By 1873 it was estimated that between two and three million acres of land had been drained. In this way, many marshy, water-logged fields were changed into rich, dry pasture. **F** shows some of the other important farming changes which took place in the nineteenth century.

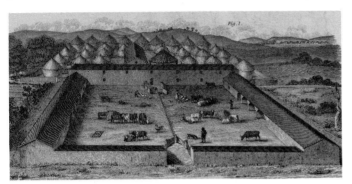

C The new Flemish farm introduced by Prince Albert

D How the Flemish farm was organized

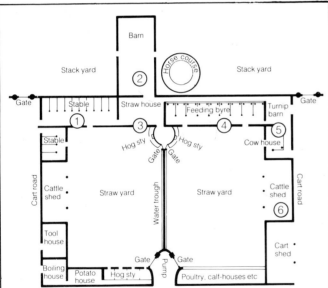

1 Horses came out of the stables (**1**) and picked up their carts.

2 The horses then carried corn from the stack-yards into the barn (**2**).

3 After threshing, the grain went into the granary (a storehouse for grain) and the straw went to the straw-barn (**3**).

4 This straw was taken to the areas that needed it (**4**, **5** and **6**).

5 After use as litter (bedding for animals), the dirty straw from the stables (**1**) and the cow stalls (**5** and **6**) was shovelled through into yards where it was trodden down before being put on the fields.

F How farming changed during the nineteenth century

Drainage
1831 James Smith of Perthshire used drains made up of shallow trenches filled with stones.
1851 Fowler's drainage plough on display at the Great Exhibition. It could lay clay pipes for only £5 an acre.

Fertilisers
1835 Guano (seagull droppings rich in phosphates) brought to Britain from Peru.
1840-1842 Justus von Liebig, a German chemist, wrote a book called *Organic Chemistry in its Applications to Agriculture* in which he showed the value of phosphates and fertilisers in farming.
1842 Sir John Lawes and Joseph Gilbert opened a factory in London to make artificial fertilisers including superphosphates.
1860 Nitrates produced in Britain.
Potash brought into Britain from Germany.

Livestock
1830s Selective breeding improved. Bakewell's ideas (see chapter 6) were used to breed cows which gave plenty of milk.
1835 Linseed and oilseed used as food for cattle.

Societies and organisations
1838 The Royal Agricultural Society set up to try to persuade farmers to farm in a more scientific way.
1842 Sir John Lawes started a research station on his family estates at Rothamstead, Hertfordshire.
1846 The Royal College of Agriculture opened at Cirencester.

New machinery
From 1830s Railways carried cattle, vegetables and corn from farms to growing towns. They carried supplies such as fertilisers, cattle-cake, seeds and machinery to farms. (See also chapter 17).

??????????????????

1 a What can you see at points **1 – 6** in **B**?
b In what ways do the model farms shown in **B** and **C** differ?
c Why do you think the farm shown in **C** and described in **D** was called a *Flemish* farm?

2 How much money was saved by using the machine-made pipes, according to **E**?

3 Using chart **F**, say whether the following statements are, *true* or *false*:
a Guano consisted of seagull droppings which had accumulated along the coastline of Peru.
b Many of Robert Bakewell's ideas were not implemented until a century after his death.
c The growth of the railway network in the 1830s helped British farmers in several different ways.
d Liebig, a German, wrote a book in the 1840s showing the value of nitrates and potash in farming.

17 The Golden Age of Farming (2)

In the 1980s we use many machines to save us time, money and labour. If you turn back to chart **F** in chapter 16, you will see that the introduction of new farm machinery was one factor which led to increased output and greater profits and hence to 'the golden age of farming'.

In the early nineteenth century very few machines were used on farms. As time passed, the use of machines slowly spread to most farms. **A** shows when different machines were introduced.

B and **C** show a steam-driven reaping machine of 1851 and a steam thresher of 1860. Many farmers bought or hired these machines and those listed in **A** believing that they could save money. It was more expensive for farmers to employ labourers using traditional tools like the sickle and scythe. For example, it took one farm labourer five days to cut, sheaf and stack an acre of wheat using a saw-edge sickle and two and a half days to do the same job using a scythe. A reaper like **B** could do the same job in half a day! The need to use fewer men and to hold down costs became even more important for farmers after 1835 when wages rose. Between 1838 and 1880, the amount produced by farmers went up by 70 per cent whereas the number of workers on the land remained about the same.

The arrival of a new machine in a small country town could cause a sensation. Thomas Hardy, a famous writer, described what happened when a seed-drill was put on display in the market-place in 1850:

‘ It was the new agricultural machine called a horse-drill, then unknown in this part of the country where the seed basket was still used for sowing. Its arrival created about as much sensation in the market-place as a flying machine

A The introduction of farm machinery

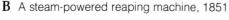

1835-1850	*Simple machines:* corn-dressers, chaff-cutters, root-slicers, bean-mills, oat-crushers, seed-drills (see chapter 4), horse-powered threshers. *Tools:* iron frame ploughs with cast-iron shares, tined cultivators, zig-zagged harrows, the 'Crosskill' and 'Cambridge' rollers.
1850-1880	*Machines:* steam thresher and mechanical harvester (by Hussey and McCormick), horse- or water-powered threshers used in north and west of England.
1880-1890	*Machines:* self-binding reapers and double-furrowed ploughs. *Tools:* improve as iron and steel industries expand.

B A steam-powered reaping machine, 1851

C An 1860s steam engine and threshing machine

would create at Charing Cross. The farmers crowded round it, women drew near it, children crept under and into it. The machine was painted in bright shades of green, yellow and red and the whole thing looked like a mixture of hornet, grasshopper and shrimp combined and magnified enormously. **9 (D)**

Some farmers were against the introduction of machines like the seed-drill. The opposition to new ideas meant that even by the end of the nineteenth century, many of the old ways of farming survived in many areas. On dairy farms, for example, there was very little change. On other farms, however, nearly all harvesting and barn work was done by machine by 1890:

The most remarkable feature of agriculture today (1885) is without a doubt the rapid introduction and use of small and portable steam engines for agricultural purposes, especially in connection with the combined threshing, straw-stacking and dressing machines, unknown until the past few years, on account of the non-efficiency of 'horse-power' to the working of such machinery. **9 (E)**

With the help of these machines, many farm labourers were saved some of the toil and sweat with which farm work had always been associated.

???????????????????

1 a Make a list of all the machines you have used today.
b State how each one has saved you time or labour.
c Take *two* of the machines listed in **A** and say how each one saved the farmer time, labour or money.
d What would be the disadvantages of using machines like **B** and **C** on a farm?

2 The year is 1870. You have decided to introduce the following machines onto your small farm in Norfolk:
One steam-threshing machine (hired)
Two turnip cutters
One seed drill
Write a speech explaining this decision to your farm workers. You should mention: time, labour, wages, profits, jobs, crops, rotations.
What arguments might you expect your farm workers to use *against* the use of machines?

3 Why are the years 1840-1870 often called 'the golden age of British farming'? Outline the main technical changes in agriculture between these years.

18 The Great Depression

You have probably heard or seen a lot about 'depression' and 'recession' in the economy on the news recently. The period 1870-1914 is known as 'the great depression'. There was a slump in agriculture and industry at the same time. Between 1870 and 1914 less arable land was cultivated, rents fell and about 300 000 farm workers left the land. Britain became a country which had to rely on imported food rather than food grown at home. The repeal of the Corn Laws meant that food was brought into Britain without any import duties or taxes being paid on it. 'The great depression' was due to a combination of bad weather, bad luck, changes in the economy and competition from abroad. **A** shows what happened.

Graph **B** shows the price of wheat and graph **C** the chief suppliers of wheat to Britain between 1840 and 1900.

The bad weather played an important part in the depression. The official Agricultural Records for the year 1879 state:

'August was very unfavourable. Pastures on clay land were as wet as in the middle of winter. Grass was all trod-

A Main causes of the Great Depression

Development	Significance	Result
Improvements in transport (railways and steamships)	More farm produce exported from USA and Europe	More wheat imported into Britain from USA and Europe
		The price of wheat fell (1874: 55 shillings a quarter; 1904: 27 shillings a quarter)
Refrigeration on ships Canning and compressed meat factories in USA	More meat brought to Britain from USA, Argentina, Australia, New Zealand	Meat prices dropped between 1870 and 1895
Low rents and rates for farms in Britain	Many farm workers and farmers badly off	Some farmers eventually ruined Many farm workers left the land
Bad weather 1873-1879 (1879 wettest ever recorded)	Diseases spread rapidly: Liver rot in sheep Foot and mouth in cattle Blight and mildew on crops	Lower production and profits; more imported beef, mutton, grain

B Price of wheat per quarter 1840-1900 (in shillings)

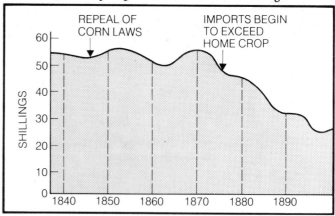

den away and cattle sunk in to their knees. The quality of both wheat and barley was wretched. No corn to sell and nobody cared to buy British produce. Vast quantities of grain pouring in from USA. In this year, the first shipment of refrigerated beef arrived in Britain.' **(D)**

E shows some meat from Australia being unloaded in 1880. How did the crisis in agriculture affect British farmers? One farmer who recorded how the crisis affected him was Mr Kendall of Somerset. This is what he wrote in 1879:

'A very heavy rainfall began in the early spring which continued without stopping until the end of September. Yet no flooding took place except in the lowland districts although every foot of clay on heavy soils or subsoil was both rotten and sodden, indeed filled with water. . . . These continuous downpours accompanied by a damp, dank, cold atmosphere which struck a chill almost into one's bones brought ruined crops with widespread

C Chief suppliers of wheat to Britain 1840-1900

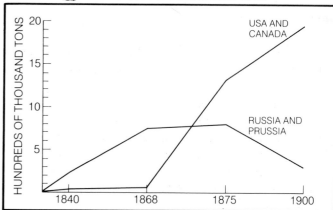

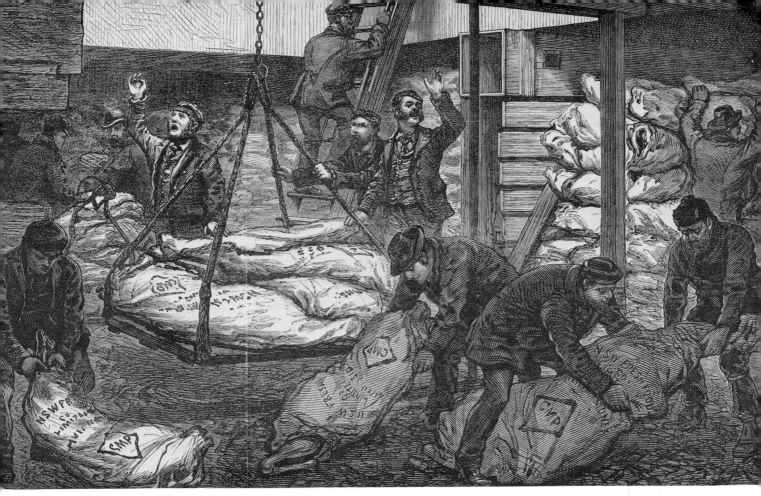

E Unloading frozen meat, imported from Australia

devastation. . . . . All mechanical work in the fields was blocked by the water and the mud which often lay just below the level of the stubble of the grass.

Barley went to the dogs badly in June and on rather heavy land disappeared in July. It first turned yellow, then faded away. Wheat, instead of ripening, turned blighty and black and seemed to shrink back like the barley two months earlier. . . .

Towards the end of September, the disastrous weather came to an end, leaving too many of us with ricks of mouldy hay; corn stacks hardly worth the threshing; our sheep folds too often wiped out or badly depleted and the farmers' bank balance seriously on the wrong side. . . . . **(F)**

Although Farmer Kendall paints a black picture of his farming year, some farmers were doing quite well for themselves. These were the men who had few acres of arable land, who hired few labourers and who could satisfy the growing demand for meat and milk from people in the towns. Milk and meat consumption doubled between 1860 and 1900. Farmers who could produce plenty of meat, milk, potatoes, hay, eggs and fresh vegetables remained fairly well off right the way through the depression.

??????????????????

1 Describe what would happen to the machines shown in chapter 17 under the sort of conditions described in **F**.

2 Using **D** and **F**, write a farmer's diary for the year 1879. You should mention what happened on your farm in March, June, July, August and September.

3 If you had been a farmer working an arable farm in 1879, how would you have coped with the problem of heavy rainfall? Would you have:

    a cut your losses and abandoned all hope of making a profit in 1879?

    b switched from arable to dairy farming or vegetable production?

    c sold your farm and land and looked for another job?

    d paid for an expensive drainage scheme?

Describe how you came to your decision.
Were there any other options open to you?

4 Using the evidence and the text say why there was a depression in British agriculture after 1870. What were the main effects of the depression?

19 The Decline of Farming

In 1879 the government set up a commission to look at the state of agriculture in Britain. The extract below is part of its report, written in 1882.

❛ There is agreement as to the extent of the distress which has fallen upon the agricultural community. Owners and occupiers have alike suffered from it. All without distinction have been involved in a general calamity.

5 *The two most prominent causes are bad seasons and foreign competition, aggravated by the increased cost of production and the heavy losses of livestock. Formerly the farmer, affected by a succession of bad seasons, was compensated by a higher price for a smaller yield; he has had in*
10 *recent years to compete with an unusually large supply at greatly reduced prices.*

On the other hand, he has had the advantage of an extended supply of feeding stuffs, such as Indian corn, linseed and cotton cakes and of artificial manures
15 *imported from abroad.*

Labour has been more costly, so that the average labour bill of an arable farm is at least twenty-five per cent higher than it was twenty-five years ago; from the competition of other industries the labouring class has been scarcely, if at
20 *all, affected by the distress which has fallen so heavily upon owners as well as occupiers. Provisions have been cheap and employment abundant, while wages in a few districts only have been slightly reduced. ❜*

---

1 What is a calamity? (line 4)

2 What is meant by owners and occupiers? (line 2)

3 What were the four main causes of the calamity?

4 What evidence is there in the passage to suggest that there had been bad harvests over a number of years?

5 Write down four imports mentioned in the passage.

6 Would these imports have helped arable or dairy farmers?

7 If a farmer's weekly wage bill had averaged out at £20 a week in 1857, what would he have had to pay out in wages each week in 1882?

8 How had the depression affected farm workers?

9 Name two countries which were exporting **a** wheat and **b** beef to Britain in 1882.

10 The Commissioners went on to recommend four measures which would make British farming more successful. What do you think these were?

AGRICULTURE 1880!

How would you have got on if you had been a farmer between 1870 and 1890? This game is for two to four players. You will need a die and some counters. Use the chart on the opposite page and follow the rules below.

1 At the start of the game each player buys a farm.

2 The players in turn throw a die, and move on the number of squares it shows.

3 If you land on a square marked **?** wait there. On your next turn, one of the other players asks you a question on agriculture.

If you get the answer *right* you can throw the die and move on.

If you get the *wrong* answer you must stay there until your next turn and answer another question – and so on until you get a right answer.

Write down what happens to you on each go.

4 The game ends when each player has had *ten* turns. Where have you finished up?

Rows A,B,C: Well done! You have come through the depression successfully and made a profit.

Rows D,E,F: You have done well enough to break even.

Rows G,H,I: Unfortunately you have been ruined and will have to sell your farm.

Events	
1st turn	
2nd turn	
3rd turn	
4th turn	
5th turn	
6th turn	
7th turn	
8th turn	
9th turn	
10th turn	
Final Row	
Verdict	Making profit / Breaking even / Ruined

48 Cold autumn MISS A TURN	49 Winter-sown corn killed GO BACK 3	50 Chilled beef from USA GO BACK 2	51 ?	52 Average year STAY PUT	53 You now have enough money to buy another farm	**A**
47 Good crop of barley MOVE ON 4	46 Sheep rot GO BACK 3	45 Blizzard in April GO BACK 2	44 Average year STAY PUT	43 ?	42 Plenty of turnips and rape MOVE ON 2	**B**
36 Average year STAY PUT	37 Beef from Argentina GO BACK 5	38 New Board of Agriculture set up MOVE ON 2	39 No rainfall for a month MISS A TURN	40 Hard frost in May GO BACK 1	41 ?	**C**
35 Winter starts early MISS A TURN	34 Farm blown down! GO BACK 7	33 Potash delivered to your farm MOVE ON 3	32 Average year STAY PUT	31 ?	30 Swine fever GO BACK 3	**D**
24 Not much hay MISS A TURN	25 Your sheepdog wins a prize MOVE ON 3	26 Wet spring GO BACK 2	27 ?	28 Average year STAY PUT	29 Hailstorms! GO BACK 3	**E**
23 Floods! GO BACK 2	22 Average year STAY PUT	21 ?	20 Labourers on strike GO BACK 4	19 You buy a second-hand seed-drill MOVE ON 3	18 Foot and mouth! GO BACK 4	**F**
12 Average year STAY PUT	13 ?	14 Cattle plague GO BACK 1	15 High winds GO BACK 2	16 Price of corn doubles MOVE ON 6	17 Storms! GO BACK 4	**G**
11 ?	10 Crops fail GO BACK 6	9 Good lambing season MOVE ON 3	8 Wet summer GO BACK 3	7 Average year STAY PUT	6 Mildew GO BACK 1	**H**
START YOU BUY A FARM	1 Corn crops good MOVE ON 4	2 Shortage of fodder MISS A TURN	3 Meat prices soar MOVE ON 4	4 You buy new machinery MOVE ON 5	5 Average year STAY PUT	**I**

20 Joseph Arch

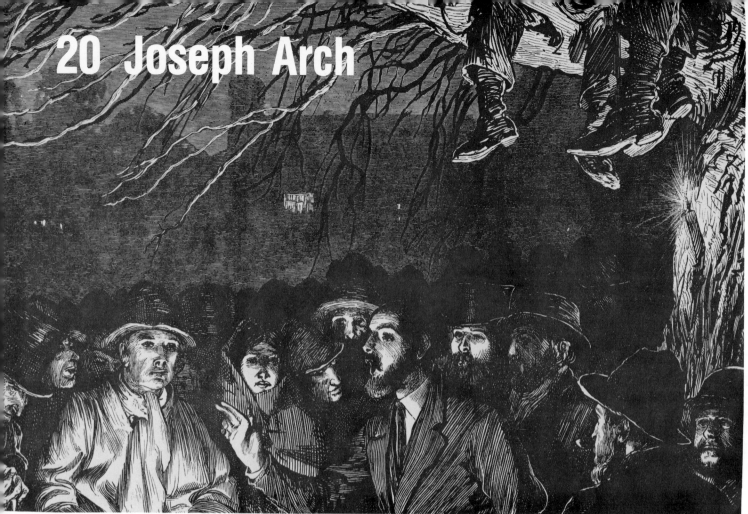

A The meeting of farm labourers at Wellesbourne

In February 1872 a meeting like **A** took place in a village in Warwickshire. Joseph Arch, a farm labourer, wrote:

❛ *When I reached Wellesbourne. . . I expected to find thirty or forty men there. . . (but) there were nearly two thousand of them. The men had come in from all the villages round within a radius of ten miles. By this time, the night had fallen pitch dark. . . in the flickering light of the lanterns I saw the earnest, up-turned faces of these poor brothers of mine — tired faces, pale with hunger and anxiety. We passed a resolution to form a union there and then and the names of the men could not be taken down fast enough. We enrolled between 200 and 300 members that night.* ❜ **(B)**

The case of the Tolpuddle Martyrs in 1834 (see chapter 14) had put many farm workers off the idea of forming unions. At the same time the increased wealth enjoyed by farmers during 'the golden age of farming' had meant that a wide social gap had grown up between many farmers and labourers. Instead of sharing the work of their men, farmers became more like factory managers. Whilst farmers seemed to be making more money, labourers seemed to be worse off than ever. In 1850, George Edwards, another farm labourer wrote:

❛ *At this time* (1850) *my father's wage had been reduced to seven shillings* (35p) *a week. The family was in terrible poverty. . . As a result of the bad food, or properly speaking the lack of food, (my mother) was only able to feed the child at her breast for one week. After the first week he had to be fed on bread soaked in very poor skimmed milk.*

At the time of my birth my father was a bullock feeder, working seven days a week, leaving home in the morning before it was light and not returning in the evening until it was dark. He never saw his children at this time except for a little while on the Sunday. The condition of the family grew worse, for although the Corn Laws were repealed in 1846, the price of food did not go down to any

D Indices of average earnings per week of agricultural labourers, 1820-1870

Date	Average earnings 1891 = 100 (base year)	Price of loaf (in old pence)
1820	95	10.1
1830	76	10.5
1840	82	10.0
1850	72	6.7
1860	89	9.1
1870	96	12.2

E Joseph Arch in 1872

extent but wages did go down. . . When the great Crimean War broke out in 1854, food rose to famine prices. . . The only thing that did not go up was wages. **)** (**C**)

Chart **D** shows the average earnings per week of agricultural labourers, between 1820 and 1870, in relation to the price in pence of a four pound loaf of bread over the same period.

Joseph Arch (**E**) became very angry about the low wages and poor conditions that many farm workers had to put up with in the 1850s and 1860s. He wrote:

(*By the end of the sixties things were so bad with the men that they were beginning to grow desperate. The men were murmuring. . . but they were afraid to speak out. . . I thought of a solution and that was combination (forming a union).*

After the harvest of 1871 had been reaped and the winter had set in, the sufferings of the men became cruel and by 1872 there seemed to be two doors open to them. One. . . led to a life of degradation in the workhouse; the other. . . (to) the grave. Their poverty had fallen to starvation point and was past all bearing. . . They saw that if they were to rise out of their miserable state, they must force open a door of escape for themselves. Oppression and hunger, and misery, made them desperate, and desperation was the mother of the union. **)** (**F**)

Arch became a famous leader of agricultural workers. **G** shows the main events in his life.

G Main events in the life of Joseph Arch

1826	Born at Barford, Warwickshire
1835	Became a crow-scarer. Wages: 4d (1½p) a day
1838	Given a job as a ploughboy. Wages: 6d (2½p)
1842	Became a mower. Paid 1s 6d (7½p) a day
1844	Became 'champion hedgecutter of England'
1847	Married and 'settled down'. Travelled up and down the country looking for farm jobs and talking to farm labourers
1870	By this time, Arch had become an expert ploughman, hurdle-maker and gate-hanger. Wages: 2s 6d (12½p) a day
1870	The Great Depression (see chapters 18-19)
1872	Farm Workers' Union formed in Warwickshire. Many strikes and lock-outs
1874	Collapse of union, mainly due to opposition of farmers and landowners
1885	Became a Liberal MP for North-West Norfolk
1900	Retired from politics
1919	Death of Joseph Arch

??????????????????

1 C describes some of the conditions George Edwards' family had to put up with in 1850.
Look at the list of benefits and list them in what you think Edwards' father would have considered the order of importance.

Child welfare benefits	Grant to improve his
Sickness benefits	cottage
Old age pensions	Local lending library
Cheaper clothing	Shorter hours of work
Cheaper food	Higher rate of pay
Improved medical care	

2 a Using **A**, **B** and the text, describe the scene at Wellesbourne that night in February 1852 as if you were a member of the crowd. You should mention: the church, the tree, the people present, lights, excitement, tension, the hopes and fears of the farm labourers.

b What do you think Arch actually said in his speech? Use **A – G** to reconstruct what he said that evening. The speech could start off like this:
''I should perhaps let you all know, right from the start, that I am a working man like yourselves. I have come here tonight to explain about something which must be sorted out between the farmers and their labourers soon. I speak of farm workers' wages.''

3 Assume it is the year 1919. You are a reporter on *The Times* and have been asked to write a short obituary notice in the paper about Joseph Arch. Using **G** as a guide, write the obituary.

21 Agricultural Trade Unions

Unions were first set up to protect the interests of workers on the land, in factories and in mines. In the eighteenth century there were two types of union. First of all, there were the *friendly societies*. These were trade clubs designed to help members with money and medical aid when they were old and sick. The second type of union was the *trade union* which aimed at raising living standards by getting wages increased, hours of work shortened and working conditions improved.

In 1750 many farm workers belonged to friendly societies, and many villages and towns in Britain had their own local friendly societies. Trade unions were another way in which workers could learn to work together and run their own affairs. The Tolpuddle Martyrs had attempted to do this in 1834 (see chapter 14). But it was not until the 1860s, a time of rising prices and unrest among factory workers, that trade unions began to interest farm workers again. Unions were formed in Buckinghamshire, Kent and Shropshire. Here, the main aim was to improve wages. In a handbill issued in 1867, the men demanded a wage of 12 shillings (60p) a week so that they could live 'not as paupers but by their own industry'. Joseph Arch's union was formed in February 1872 (see chapter 20). Once this union had been formed, the farm workers wanted to see results as quickly as possible. In March 1872, they demanded an increase in wages to 13p a day and shorter working hours. When the demands were ignored by the farmers, the labourers came out on strike. **A** shows a strike meeting in Warwickshire in 1872.

The newspapers supported the farm labourers and members of the public sent the union money. In mid-April, the labourers were given an increase in pay. One paper reported their victory like this:

Two years ago, a strike of agricultural labourers would have been thought impossible. It was believed that our clod hoppers were incapable of combination. Yet, now that a combination has been effected, that a strike has been struck, the movement has spread all over the country with marvellous rapidity. **(B)**

In May, the National Agricultural Labourers' Union (NALU) was formed.

It was the first national society ever to cater for farm workers and Joseph Arch was elected leader. It had its own newspaper, *The Labourers' Union Chronicle* which contained news and reports of its meetings. **C** shows the union's banner.

After the NALU had been formed, there was even

A Farm workers at a strike meeting in 1872

D Average earnings of agricultural labourers in England and Wales, by region

	1867-70	1898	1907
London area and home counties	16s.6d.	18s.5d.	18s.6½d.
South west	12s.5d.	15s.7d.	16s.10d.
Rural south east	14s.4½d.	15s.9d.	16s.5d.
South Wales	12s.7½d.	17s.0½d.	18s.2d.
Rural Wales and Herefordshire	13s.0d.	16s.1½d.	17s.8d.
Midlands	14s.1d.	17s.0d.	18s.4½d.
Lincolnshire, Rutland, Yorkshire (E. and N.)	17s.1d.	18s.0d.	18s.10d.
Lancashire, Cheshire, Yorkshire (W.)	17s.1d.	18s.8d.	19s.7d.
Cumberland and Westmorland	18s.6d.	18s.9d.	19s.2d.
Northumberland and Durham	18s.9d.	20s.5½d.	21s.5½d.
Average for England and Wales	13s.9d.	16s.0d.	17s.11d.

greater pressure for higher wages. In 1874 the new union faced its greatest challenge. The labourers in the small Suffolk village of Exning demanded a rise of 5p a week. The farmers' answer was to 'lock out' all union members. This meant closing down the farms and not letting the men come in for work. The strike spread to other counties and soon 6000 men were on strike. The NALU had to pay out strike money amounting to £24 000. Arch and the other union leaders could not raise sufficient funds to support the men who had been locked out and on 27 July the men were told by the union to return to work. Some men found they had been sacked in their absence, some went back on condition they did not remain members of the union and some emigrated.

After this, many labourers became discouraged and left the NALU. Bad harvests and cheap imports of grain from the USA did little to help. By 1880, membership of the union had gone down to 20 000. Joseph Arch became the Liberal MP for Norfolk and turned his attention to campaigning for agricultural workers inside Parliament. Although the NALU increased its membership in the 1880s, the 1890s was a decade of great hardship and in 1896 the union collapsed altogether. However, as **D** shows, the wages earned by farm workers had gone up during this period.

C The banner of the National Agricultural Labourers' Union

UNITED DIVIDED

WE STAND WE FALL

VE DEMAND SOCIAL LIBERTY,

LITICAL & RELIGIOUS EQUALITY

HE COMPLETE RIGHTS OF MAN.

??????????????????

1 In **A** you can see three men talking in the bottom of the picture. Write a conversation between the three men in which two of them try to persuade the third to join their union.

2 **C** shows some of the NALU's demands.
 a What demand seems to have been left off the banner?
 b Which demand refers to the fact that at this time many farm workers did not have the vote?
 c How could the farm workers have gained 'social liberty'?
 d What point are the pictures of the barrels intended to make?

3 Using **D**:
 a Draw a graph or histogram to show the increase in agricultural labourers' earnings in different regions in 1867, 1898 and 1907.
 b In which area(s) was there the greatest increase in earnings?
 c In which area(s) was there the least increase?
 d Try to account for these differences. (Clues: fewer workers, prices, fairer employers, unions, more farm produce needed)

22 A Devon Farm in 1907

We always thought of school as a bit of a nuisance. First of all I was taught at home. Then, when I was about eight, my sister and I went to school in Totnes. At a quarter to eight in the morning, the two of us walked with a candle-lit lantern to Buckfastleigh Station. We left the lantern with the station-master, caught the train to Totnes and collected the lantern again when we got back at 4.30. (A)

The boy who caught the train to Totnes was called Donald Warren. He was born and brought up at Rill Farm, near Buckfastleigh, Devon. **B** is a photograph of Donald and his family in 1907. Donald is on horseback, holding a stick.

Later in life, Donald recalled what it was like on a farm in 1907:

The farm day was regularly punctuated by meals. There were always three or four kettles of half hot water in the big fireplace. A packet of wood was laid on the fire the night before, so that this could be lit up and the water boiled quickly for the early morning cup of tea. Then it was out by 6.30 for milking, to see to the calves and to get the horses ready. Breakfast was at 7.45 and any man working outside would come in to join my father, my brother

and myself. At two minutes to eight, my father would produce his hunter out of his waistcoat pocket and say 'Are you fellows going to work today or not?' He expected us to be out on the stroke of eight, even though we'd done all the work in the yard before starting breakfast. (C)

At harvest time Donald's father had to employ extra men:

These men used to come and help with the harvest. There was no machinery then, only horses and men with pitchforks. Food and drink were a form of payment. My mother produced a large basket at midday with all the food they could want to eat, also tea and jugs of cider. They'd stay till ten o'clock at night and work. They didn't want to be paid in cash but in the winter they got potatoes, carrots, apples and so on. (D)

E shows two of the men at work harvesting. The boy on the left is Donald.

After the day's work was over, there was usually time to relax in the farmhouse. With no TV or radio, people had to think up their own amusements:

Generally speaking, there was nothing to do in the evenings. We sat there with the oil lamps on and might

B The Warren family at Rill Farm, 1907

E Donald and two farm workers in the harvest field

play cards or draughts. Nine o'clock was our bedtime with a glass of hot milk. But sometimes I did go a bit mad. I remember one August, spending the day cutting six acres of wheat, with three horses and a self-binder. I caught 120 rabbits and finished work at 9 p.m. I put away the horses, had supper, then changed, got on a bicycle, cycled nine miles to Newton Abbot Fair and home again. Then I was up and working by 6 o'clock the next morning. (F)

Donald's memories of his childhood seem to have been happy ones. Although life was hard for many people, working on the land had its rewards and compensations:

Farming was a way of life then, and although there wasn't much money in it for anyone, there was a great deal of satisfaction to be had. The men enjoyed friendly competition with each other. For example, I knew two men who would go out around August or September where we were growing mangolds (a kind of beet used as cattle food). They would have pieces of whipcord in their pockets. They used to measure the mangolds with this cord, tie a knot in it and go off to the pub where they all met on Sunday morning. They would take the cords out of their pockets and say 'I've got a mangold that size!' 'Oh no you haven't.' 'Yes, I 'ave.' Another man would produce his cord and put it out. 'You see, 'ere's a bigger one. . .' This went on from August until the time the mangolds were lifted in the autumn. Yet they weren't their own mangolds — they were only growing them for the stock where they worked. Nevertheless, they were trying to outdo each other and the fights there were over the size of this, the size of that. . . . (G)

H shows the main changes in rural life which had taken place between 1850 and 1907.

H How farm life changed between 1850 and 1907

1850	1907
Few machines used on farms (some steam-threshing machines for hire); most work done by hand	Far more machines – especially reapers and binders
Ratio of about five workers to each employer	Ratio of about three workers to each employer
1 124 000 male farm workers 143 000 female workers	674 000 male farm workers 13 500 female workers
Average wage: 12s 6d (62½p)	Average wage: 17s 11d (90p)
Most food grown locally	Meat, butter, vegetables and fruit brought from all over Britain
People travelled on foot, or by horse, wagon, trap, carrier's cart	People travelled by train, bicycle, bus – a few cars
No compulsory education – some village schools	Compulsory education to age 12, many board (state) schools
People went to county fairs, parish feasts, local celebrations	People went to football, music hall, on railway outings. Read more newspapers
Local parish constable kept law and order	County Police Forces set up (part of a national system)

??????????????????

1 If you had worked on Rill Farm in 1907, what would you have done at:
 6.00 a.m. 6.30 a.m. 7.45 a.m. 12.00 9.00 p.m.?

2 a What important point was Donald trying to make in **G**?
 b In what ways do boys and girls, men and women, have 'friendly competitions' today?

3 Look at **H**. Given a choice, would you have preferred to have been a farm worker in 1850 or 1907? Give reasons for your answer.

4 How much trust can we place on **A** to **G** as pieces of historical evidence?

23 The First World War

A Schoolboys setting out to 'dig for victory'

B Women also joined the campaign to produce more food

A shows a group of schoolboys setting off to dig up the school playing fields in order to grow food. Once the playing fields had been dug up, they were known as 'victory plots'. The government needed the boys' help because it was 1917 and Britain had been at war with Germany since 1914. Thousands of farm workers had left the land to join the army. To provide Britain with grain and vegetables, women, schoolchildren and prisoners-of-war had been asked to join a campaign to produce more food. **B** shows a woman farm worker unloading sacks of corn. In 1917, a spokesman from the Board of Agriculture said:

❛ *The large increase in production is due to the patriotic response of women of all classes to do work upon the land in the place of men on war service. Many educated women have joined in the work, and it is an inference drawn by those watching over the movement that the presence of these educated women, together with the facts that the life is really healthy and the work is now much better paid, has caused farm work to be no longer regarded as a somewhat degrading occupation for women but rather as one which is both honourable and useful.* ❜ (**C**)

When the war had started in 1914, everyone had thought that the fighting would be over in a few months. Most people were not aware of the danger of starvation facing Britain. The country had come to rely upon large amounts of imported food (**D**).

D Imports of food into Britain in 1914

Meat	40%
Cereals	80%
Fruit	75%
Sugar	100%

E Measures introduced by the government to help farmers

Date	Measure	Results
1915	Board of Education circular	Many children given permission to miss school to help farmers
1916	War Agricultural Committees	Parks and playing fields ploughed up; more arable land available
1917	Cultivation of Lands Order	Farmers forced to plough up more pasture
	Ministry of Food	Food supplies rationed
	More machinery introduced	Lorries used for shifting quantities of food; Fordson tractors brought in from USA; fewer horses and men required
	Corn Production Act	A minimum wage for labourers; more help for farmers growing wheat and oats

Unfortunately the Germans had developed a new and deadly type of submarine, the U-boat. These submarines were able to sink hundreds of merchant ships carrying grain and meat to Britain.

The government had to act quickly. To help farmers, a number of measures were introduced (E).

What were conditions like for the children who went to help the farmers? They were often paid less than one shilling (5p) a day for their labour. In Buckinghamshire in 1916, the school day started at 8 a.m. with a lunch break between 10.30 and 11.30 a.m. Teaching finished at 1.40 p.m. and the children went off to work on nearby farms. Some pupils were asked to collect horse-chestnuts and blackberries for the farmers. The chestnuts were used to make a type of flour and the blackberries were made into jam for the soldiers.

In some country towns and villages, children were more aware of the war than in others. John Moore described what he saw when he was seven years old:

The people cheered the soldiers all the way to the station. Those farmers' sons, gamekeepers, poachers and hobbledehoys went on to play soldiers in Flanders for the better part of five years. They were maimed, blinded, and slain. But after the soldiers had gone, it was a long time before the war began to have any effect on Elmbury. My mother collected vegetables for the navy; and I remember the garden looking like a harvest festival, with piles of cauliflowers, cabbages, lettuces, beets and marrows on their way to Scapa Flow. Two young women dressed themselves up in green jerseys and tight breeches and went off to work on the land. Everyone was shocked by this tomboyish gesture. The trousers were regarded as the height of indecency. (F)

In other country areas, the war had very little effect. One farmer wrote:

A lot of us farmers hid our horses in the Great War, when the officers came round. The officers always gave

good money for a horse but sometimes the horses were like brothers and the farmers couldn't bear to let them go, so they hid them. I wasn't called up. Nothing happened to me and I didn't remind them. We didn't really miss the men who didn't come back. The village stayed the same. If there were changes, I never felt them, so I can't remark upon them. (G)

As a result of the government's emergency measures, Britain was producing more food than ever by 1918. The war had brought misery to millions but prosperity to farming.

???????????????????

1 **E** shows measures taken by the government to save Britain from starvation.

   a Why do you think no new measures were taken in 1914?

   b Which of the measures do you think was most important? Why?

   c Can you think of *three* other ways in which the government could have protected our food supplies?

2 Extracts **F** and **G** describe the effects of the First World War on people's lives.

   a What similarities are there between what the two extracts say about the effects of the war?

   b What differences are there?

   c How do you explain these differences and similarities?

3 Imagine the headmaster of your school has just told your class that for the next year or so you will be missing certain lessons each week to work on the land. Your initial reaction is probably one of pleasure. But after a few minutes you begin to have doubts. List the advantages and disadvantages, writing as many items in each column as you can.

24 The Slump

E Labourers in the harvest field, 1922

Len Thompson was a Suffolk farm worker who had fought in World War I. When he returned from Germany he wrote:

❛ The soldiers who got back to the village recovered very quickly. We were thankful that it was all over and we could get back to our work. Yet things had changed and people were different. The farm workers who had been soldiers were looked at in a new way. We felt that there must be no slipping back to the bad old ways and in about 1920 we formed a branch of the Agricultural Workers' Union. ❜ **(A)**

Joseph Arch's union (see chapter 21) had collapsed in 1896 but had been revived in 1906. In 1921 another economic slump took place. Prices dropped and many farmers faced ruin. According to Len Thompson:

❛ 1920 looked like a very good year. We were getting 38 shillings and sixpence (£1.92½) a week on the farms. We worked 54 hour a week and had a half-holiday and if we worked overtime it was another 1/1d (5½p) an hour. The farmers were able to pay the new wages because of the Corn Act (see chapter 23). The slump set in during the great hot summer of 1921. We had no rain from March right through to October. The corn didn't grow no more than a foot high and most of it didn't come to the ear. We harvested what we could and the last loads were leaving the fields when we heard 'the wages are coming down this week'. It was true. The farmers told the men that they were cutting their pay. ❜ **(B)**

Until 1920 the government had been willing to pay a subsidy to farmers. This meant that the farmers would always receive a fair price for their produce and could therefore pay their labourers reasonable wages. In 1920 however, these payments came to an end. Soon farm workers' wages had been cut to 27 shillings and sixpence a week (£1.37½) Len Thompson blamed it all on the government:

❛ It was the government's fault. They ended the Corn Act too soon. They said it was best if the farmers made their own bargains which meant that they wouldn't pay the subsidies. The price of wheat was quartered in a year. Cattle were sold for next to nothing. The farmers became broke and frightened, so they took it out on us men. We reminded them that we had fought in the war and they reminded us that they had too. So it was hate all round. ❜ **(C)**

The final blow came when Len's union collapsed a few months later:

❛ Then we had to close down our union because nobody could afford to pay the 4d a week membership fee. I remember the week this happened. I drew 27 shillings and sixpence from the farmers and after I had given my wife 24 shillings and paid my union 4d and my rent 3 shillings and a penny, I had a penny left. So I threw it across the field. I'd worked hard. A penny was what a child had. I wasn't having that. I would sooner have nothing. ❜ **(D)**

F Changes that took place in Foxton between 1901 and 1941

Year	Population	Houses	Farmers	Farm Workers	Horses	Tractors	Combines
1901	426	72	8	45	35	0	0
1911	481	94	8	35	32	0	0
1921	480	98	8	34	32	1	0
1931	469	122	8	31	29	7	0
1941	490	123	7	30	25	18	0

As the slump got worse, many farm-workers became unemployed. Some left the land for good. **E** shows a group of farm labourers, like Len and his friends, in 1922.

Not far from Len Thompson's village in Suffolk, lies the village of Foxton in Cambridgeshire. Rowland Parker, a writer who lives in Foxton, drew up a table of statistics to show what had happened to the village between 1901 and 1941 (**F**).

How did Rowland Parker build up this table of statistics? He had to look at official census returns (population counts) or actual counts held in the village. The rest of the figures are *estimates* based on what older people could remember. Taken as a whole, the figures give us a picture of what a typical Cambridgeshire village was like between the wars. Chart **G** shows some of the effects of the First World War on agriculture as a whole.

G The impact of the First World War on agriculture

Event	Result
3 million acres of land added to the area cultivated	A great increase in the production of wheat, barley, oats, potatoes, hay, root crops
World-wide trade depression	Fewer people willing to buy produce; lower prices; a depression in British agriculture. (e.g. Wheat fell in price from 86/4d per quarter in 1920 to 40/9d in 1922)
Higher costs (machinery, labour, buildings)	Some farmers went bankrupt in the 1920s
Government measures (e.g. Agricultural Wages Board 1924 – to provide farm workers with a living wage)	Increased wages for farm workers – up to 30/- (£1.50) a week in some areas
Scientific and technical advances made during the war	More tractors, milking machines, pest controls, weed killers
Acts of Parliament (e.g. Agricultural Credit Act 1928 – to provide credit for farm improvements)	Loans for farmers; lower guaranteed prices for wheat; greater security of tenure

??????????????????

1 Compare Len Thompson's weekly budget in 1920 (**D**) with the farm labourer's weekly budget in 1795 (chapter 10). Draw a table like the one below:

	1795	1920
Weekly wage Rent Amount spent on food, clothing etc.		

2 a In **E**, match up numbers **1 – 5** with the following:
the 'sweep' (pulled along by a shire horse);
the horse which worked the "elevator";
the shire horse;
the stack;
the 'elevator' (designed to place hay on top of stack).
b At what time of year was this photo taken?
c How do you think the hay from the 'sweep' was thrown into the elevator?
d How many men and children were involved in this task?

3 Look at the table of statistics in **F**. The following questions are based on the statistics.
a What was the percentage increase in tractors in the village between 1931 and 1941?
b Is it true to say that the decline in the number of horses used was a result of the increased number of tractors?
c How do you explain the fact that although the population of Foxton increased by 64 between 1901 and 1941, the number of farm-workers decreased by 15?
d What was the ratio of farmers to farm-workers in 1901? What was the ratio in 1941?
e How do you explain the fact that between 1931 and 1941 the number of people in the village increased by 21, yet the number of houses increased by 1?
f Combine harvesters had been invented early in the twentieth century, yet none appear to have been used on farms in Foxton during this period. Can you think of a reason for this?

25 Between the Wars

A A 1936 Ferguson tractor

On visits to the countryside, you may have been surprised at the large number of expensive machines used by farmers. Many of these machines first appeared on farms between 1918 and 1939. **A** is a photograph of a tractor produced by Ferguson in 1936. The years between the two World Wars saw a greater number of machines in use on farms than ever before. **B** shows the different kinds of machinery used and the type of work done.

The first tractors of the 1880s had pulled the old horse-drawn harrows and drills along behind them. In 1925 Harry Ferguson, an Irishman, designed a tractor, the TE 20, which was later used all over the world. The most important feature of the Ferguson tractor was its three-point linkage. This was a new method of hitching up ploughs and drills to a mechanical arm behind the tractor. The tractor and plough then became one mechanical unit. It made ploughing much easier and meant that the tractor could back right up to a hedge, leaving no gap between the plough-land and hedgerow at all. **C** shows the number of tractors, horses and farm workers 1916-52.

The second type of machine to appear at this time was the combine harvester. These were first built in the 1920s and carried out harvest work much more quickly than had previously been possible. **D** shows how a combine harvester works.

The third machine to appear was the milking machine. A machine of the 1890s had used a pipeline connected to the farmyard pump to draw milk from the cow's udder. This had not worked properly because when a calf takes milk from its mother, there is suction and then gentle pressure on the teat of the udder as the calf closes its

B Farm machinery in use between the wars

Machine	Work done
Tractor	Towing: trailers, ploughs, harrows, reapers, drills Driving: stationary equipment (with a pulley) Pulling: logs, bales of straw, 'sweeps'
Combine harvester	Harvesting, threshing, sorting and drying grain in one operation. Also used for grass, clover, peas, rape, maize
Milking machines	Milking large numbers of cows in as short a time as possible

C Numbers of tractors, horses and farm workers, 1916-1952

Year	Tractors	Farm horses	Farm workers
1916	1000	1 000 000	1 000 000
1921	6000	955 000	996 000
1939	50 000	649 000	711 000
1942	101 000	585 000	824 000
1946	180 000	519 000	889 000
1952	325 000	254 000	804 000

D How the combine harvester works

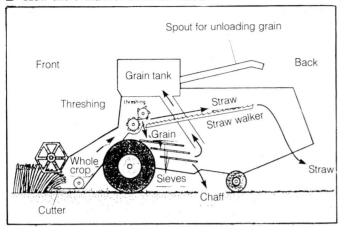

mouth to suck and relaxes it to swallow. The machine of 1892 had provided suction only. A Scotsman, Alexander Shields, invented a device which caused a break in the suction, in the same way a calf would behave in natural feeding. This device was used in the milking machines of the 1930s. **E** is a photo of a milking machine being used in 1935.

There was so much more food being produced by the new machines that the government set up organizations

E Using a milking machine in the 1930s

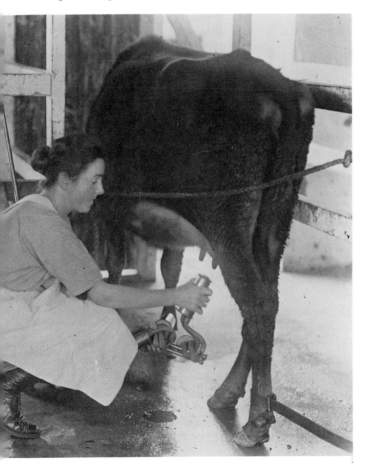

to control output and prices. These were called *marketing boards*. **F** shows how the marketing boards worked.

Although some farmers disliked the idea of the marketing boards, it did mean that they were certain to get a fair price for their produce. Fewer farmers faced the prospect of ruin in difficult times.

F An outline of the 1931 Agricultural Marketing Act

1 Marketing boards to be set up to control price and output of milk, hops, potatoes, bacon, pork.
2 The marketing boards to be made up of groups of producers from all over the country.
3 The boards to limit the amount that farmers could produce to prevent too much food flooding the market at any one time.
4 The boards to pay farmers a guaranteed price for their produce.
5 All farmers to sell their produce through the boards.
6 The boards to restrict the import of foreign food if necessary.

??????????????????

1 Using the evidence, the text, and your knowledge of agriculture answer the questions below:
  a In what way was the TE 20 a breakthrough in tractor design?
  b Why do you think there were a lot of tractor deaths in the 1930s?
  c Write down *three* types of farm work a tractor can be used for. In what ways was the tractor better than other tools and machines?
  d Why was the combine superior to the old machines used for harvesting?
  e How was milking carried out before milking machines were introduced?

2 Look at **F**.
  a Which item, 1–6 was most difficult for the marketing boards to enforce?
  b Why do you think some farmers disliked the idea of marketing boards?

3 **C** shows a 'horses versus tractors' statistical table, 1916-52.
  a Draw a bar chart or histogram to show the number of tractors, horses and farm workers on farms between 1939 and 1952.
  b What sort of crop was grown to feed horses?
  c What sort of farm work do horses still do?
  d How do you think the tractor has changed the life of the farm labourer?

26 The Farm in the Fens

In 1938, Alan Bloom bought Priory Farm in Cambridgeshire for £1600. The farm consisted of 200 acres of reed-beds surrounding derelict buildings. Alan wrote:

The cottage was of the usual drab brick. Large cracks had been cemented up and aginst the corners were brick buttresses. . . the chimney had a bend in it and the front door was fitted askew. Odd sheets of corrugated iron on the buildings close by flapped noisily in the wind. . . Inside these buildings were several pigs, two horses and a few steers — and plenty of wet muck. There was no cart or implement shed; carts, rakes, horse-hoes and ploughs lay around the straw stacks. **(A)**

The Fens are a marshy, low-lying part of East Anglia. Alan's first task was to plough up rough grazing land. A farm hand, George Johnson, did the job, using two horses and a single-furrowed plough. He asked Alan whether he should 'square plough' the field:

You see, if you plough round a piece in the middle of a field, you finish up next the ditch and there 'eent no deep open furrows anywhere 'cept round the outsides and tha's where the highest part of the field is 'cause of where stuff from the ditches bin throwed out. **(B)**

The next problem was drainage. Many of the ditches and dykes on Priory Farm were blocked up and in need of

C Digging drainage ditches on Priory Farm

attention. Two local men were brought to the farm to dig ditches to carry water away from the fields. C shows them at work. Alan described what happened:

George and Stuart set about ditching. . . using a flat, heart-shaped moor spade for cutting the sides neatly down, sloping inwards to form a firm 'batter' (sloping wall). A frog-nosed shovel did the excavating, while a light wooden scoop was used for the slub (mud) in the bottom. They took each ditch at piece-work rates at ten shillings a chain length. . . But the water would not run away. One man said 'Rather have hoigh any day than this 'ere old fen.' George said 'The ole land wants clay, it dew. No use farming against water.' **(D)**

Field ditches had previously been dug to carry the water into *interlines* (secondary ditches), which ran into the main drains. From here, the water was pumped up to river level. Unfortunately, only half the Fen was being properly drained because the main drains had become blocked up over the years.

Alan decided to get the Burwell Drainage Commissioners to help him improve his land, but they lacked the money to help him. A few months later one of Alan's horses fell into a drainage ditch, and died because the drain had no solid bottom.

Sid and I, who were forking beet into the barge, heard a shout and the sound of breaking timber. We raced down, and there was the cart, wheels uppermost in the drain, its shafts pinning down the horse, of which we could see nothing but the flanks protruding above the water. There was hardly any movement, but, farther out, bubbles were rising to the top of the black, muddy water. Sid scrambled out on the upturned cart, but, clutching hold of the wheel, up to his knees in water, he still could not reach the mare's head.

Poor Sid was frantic, and so was George Johnson who was nearby. They did not care if they got up to their necks if only they could save that horse but it was hopeless from the start. The mare was dead, and had her muzzle deep in the mud on the bottom. **(E)**

To improve his land, Alan had to have better drainage but the Commissioners and the government were still unwilling or unable to help him. Alan was only saved from ruin by the outbreak of World War II (see chapter 27). He wrote:

. . . the war which brought death and destruction to so many has saved me and others. We were harvesting on

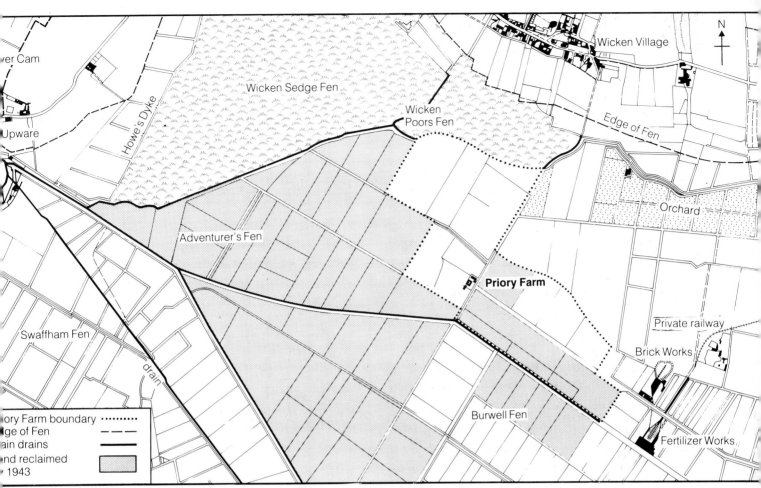

G Priory Farm and Adventurer's Fen in 1943, showing the increase in cultivated areas

Map legend:
- ...ory Farm boundary ············
- ...ge of Fen – – –
- ...ain drains ——
- ...nd reclaimed [shaded]
- ... 1943

Map labels: ...ver Cam, Wicken Village, Wicken Sedge Fen, Howe's Dyke, Upware, Wicken Poors Fen, Edge of Fen, Adventurer's Fen, Orchard, Priory Farm, Swaffham Fen, drain, Private railway, Brick Works, Burwell Fen, Fertilizer Works, N

---

that Friday when Sid's wife came out and told us that Poland had been attacked. Except for a few brief sentences in which the men expressed their opinions of Hitler and Germany, very little was said for the rest of the day and the usual harvest chaffing and chattering was absent. **(F)**

Shortly after war had been declared, a man from the Ministry of Agriculture visited Priory Farm. The need to produce more home-grown food in wartime (see chapter 27) meant that as much land as possible needed to be reclaimed and cultivated. A War Agricultural Committee decided to drain Adventurers Fen as part of a new drainage scheme and new concrete roads were laid. Soon Priory Farm was producing plenty of sugar-beet, wheat, oats, barley and potatoes. Three years later, Alan was able to write:

The worries of reclamation, of fighting and overcoming obstacles to the plough and the seed-drill were over. Adventurers Fen and Priory Farm had proved that crops equal to any other of the black fens could be grown. Those ideas and hopes that I'd held at the back of my mind

could now begin to emerge. More complete fertility, extended mechanisation, more and better buildings, a thorough livestock policy, alternate leys (fields) to give some much-cropped land a rest. But had it not been for the war, the hopes I had for Priory Farm might well have been submerged below the fen, never to rise again. **(H)**

??????????????????

1 a How do you think Priory Farm got its name?
b 'No use farming against water', said the farm hand in **D**. What did he mean by this?
c Why was the land around Priory Farm so difficult to drain?

2 How did Priory Farm differ from the Devon Farm in chapter 22?

3 Refer to map **G**.
a How did the landscape around Priory Farm change between 1939 and 1943?
b Try to account for these changes.

27 The Second World War

You may have parents or grandparents who lived through the Second World War (1939-1945). For many people it was a frightening experience.

In 1939, when the war began, Britain was importing 70 per cent of its food. Soon U-boats were sinking large numbers of merchant ships. Britain had to produce far more food at home.

Fortunately, the government made more careful plans than before the First World War (see chapter 23). A Ministry of Food was set up. The aim was to provide enough food for everyone. Grassland was again ploughed up and more crops were grown. Farmers were paid a subsidy of £2 an acre if they were prepared to plough up grassland which had remained unploughed for seven years. It is hardly surprising that many farmers once more became very prosperous!

The County War Agricultural Committees were set up again (see chapter 23). They gave farmers advice. They had many powers and could even tell a farmer which crops he should grow. They provided money, fertilisers and labour. More ·tractors, lorries, vans and combine harvesters were used to produce the best results possible. Soon, the amount of land under cultivation increased from five million to eight million hectares.

To make sure that everyone received their fair share of food, ration books were issued by the Ministry of Food.

A A week's food rations

B Land girls from the Wolverhampton Women's Land Army

D Allotments in the moat of the Tower of London

E Effect of the Second World War on yields per acre

Date	Wheat (bushels)	Barley (bushels)	Oats (bushels)	Potatoes (tons)	Turnips and Swedes (tons)	Mangolds (tons)	Sugar-Beet (tons)
1935	33.5	34.7	44.9	6.3	12.2	18.8	9.1
1940	34.6	38.3	47.8	8.5	14.5	18.3	11.1
1945	60.3	59.2	63.7	16.2	26.4	36.5	18.6

Sugar, meat, milk, butter, cooking fat and other items were rationed. People were only allowed a certain amount of each type of food each week. **A** shows ration books and the amount of food each person was allowed a week.

In this war, the government did not rely solely on prisoners-of-war and children to help farmers. Women were encouraged to join the Women's Land Army. The 'land girls' were expected to live on farms. They did the work of the thousands of farm labourers who had joined the army, navy and air force. **B** is a photograph of the Wolverhampton Women's Land Army in 1942.

One woman who joined the Women's Land Army said:

❛ Our training lasted about six weeks. We stayed in a hostel near Woodstock in Oxfordshire. I was taught to drive a tractor and trailer. When a farmer needed a tractor-driver, I went out to his farm. We had to get up early each day, at about 6 a.m. We needed a big breakfast of porridge and dried egg. Then there were our sandwiches to prepare for lunch-time.

I often had to cycle 12 or 14 miles in the dark to get to work. It was marvellous working out in the open air but it was sometimes very tiring. Many of the girls found the fumes from the tractors too much to cope with.

One of the worst jobs was putting bands around the wheels of the tractors when we wanted to drive along roads. We had to jack each wheel up which was exhausting. The tractor-work was mainly ploughing, drilling corn and cutting grass but sometimes the girls would help the farmer with milking and sheep-shearing.

Our uniform consisted of a land army hat, twill dungarees, breeches, a tie and a thick mac. For entertainment we had to rely on invitations to air-force bases where they sometimes had dances at the week-ends. ❜ (C)

The work done by the Women's Land Army, the Ministry of Food and the Agricultural Committees led to a great increase in produce per acre. By 1943, for example, nearly twice as much land was under cultivation compared to 1939. Even parks and gardens were turned into allotments to grow food (**D**). More important, over twice as much food was being produced by that land. **E** shows the average yield per acre of certain crops between 1935 and 1945.

The great increase in production brought prosperity to British farming. By 1945, at the end of the war, the average price obtained for wheat had gone up from 21s 5d (£1.07) per quarter to 64s 10d (£3.24). More animals were being raised on farms than ever before. The farmers hoped that the good times would continue for them after the war was over. Chart **F** shows some of the results of the government measures to help farmers in the Second World War.

F Government measures to help farmers

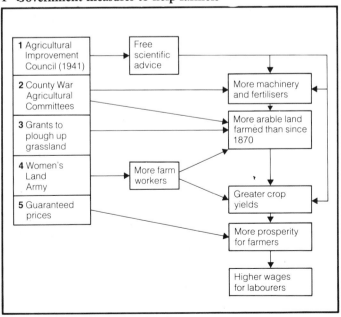

1 Agricultural Improvement Council (1941) → Free scientific advice

2 County War Agricultural Committees

3 Grants to plough up grassland

4 Women's Land Army → More farm workers

5 Guaranteed prices

More machinery and fertilisers

More arable land farmed than since 1870

Greater crop yields

More prosperity for farmers

Higher wages for labourers

???????????????????

1 Use **A** to work out roughly how much of the following items people were allowed each week when food was rationed.

a milk		**f** bacon	
b sugar		**g** jam	
c eggs		**h** butter	
d cheese		**i** cooking fat	
e tea		**j** meat	

2 Design a poster *either* aimed at encouraging women to join the WLA *or* showing the amount of rations each adult was to be allowed each week.

28 1945-1970

It was January 1947. The worst blizzard for forty years had struck Britain. All over the country thousands of sheep and cattle were dying in huge snowdrifts. At one farm over 150 sheep were lost. Farm tractors had to be used to get food supplies through to isolated villages. In many areas food production ground to a halt.

At the end of this dreadful winter the government took steps to help farmers. Politicians were worried in case agriculture went into serious decline as it had done after the wars with France (1793-1815) and the First World War (1914-1918). An Agriculture Act was passed in 1947 which outlined a farming policy for the 1950s and '60s. Farmers were to be guaranteed a fair price for their farm produce, and this price would be reviewed every year. Grants and subsidies would be given to farmers to encourage them to use up-to-date methods, such as the use of fertilisers and lime. A National Agricultural Advisory Service would also be set up, to advise farmers about soils, crops, cattle and farm management.

The Agriculture Act led to more food being produced at less cost. New farm buildings were put up and machinery, cold stores, milking machines and combine harvesters were bought. Farmers purchased greater numbers of tractors. By the 1950s so many tractors were being used that the number of working horses went down rapidly. **A** shows the decline in horses and numbers of farm workers, 1946-1968, as the number of tractors increased.

A Numbers of tractors, horses and farm workers 1946-1968

Year	Tractors	Horses	Farm workers
1946	180 000	519 000	889 000
1952	325 000	254 000	804 000
1958	431 000	84 000	670 000
1965	500 000	21 000	514 000
1968	500 000	5000	453 000

The countryside began to change. As fields became larger for the use of new machinery, our hedgerows began to disappear. **B** shows what happened to fields and hedges between 1945 and 1970.

Farmers are still destroying hedges at the rate of 5000 miles a year. If this continues, Britain will be without hedges in a hundred years. **C** shows a hedge planted on a bank thrown up from a ditch. On either side of most hedges is a grassy verge. These vary in width.

B How fields and hedges changed between 1945 and 1970

	1945	1970
Average field size (in acres)	19	45
Length of hedge per acre (in yards)	95	58
Hedgerow trees per 100 acres	59	12

Professor Hoskins, a famous historian, has written:

In some parts of England, such as East Anglia, the bulldozer rams at the old hedges and blots them out to make fields big enough for the machines of the new ranch-farming and the business-men farmers of five to ten thousand acres. Fortunately, the tractor and bulldozer cannot easily destroy the great hedgebanks; nor is it worth doing, for the good farmer knows the value of these banks as shelter, and of the hedges for timber. Much of the old field pattern therefore remains with its tangle of deep lanes and thick hedges. **(D)**

Farm buildings have also changed. Today, a modern farmyard will contain machinery such as combine harvesters and grain driers worth thousands of pounds. Most milking is done by machine and there have to be high standards of hygiene and cleanliness. At the same time many farmworkers have lost their jobs as more and more machines are used (see **A**). Today there are under 500 000 farm workers in Britain. The size of farms, however, has steadily increased:

The number of holdings has been halved since 1920, resulting in an increase in the average farm size from 122 to 317 acres. Some farmers, however, farm several holdings and the average amount of land worked by farmers exceeds 1000 acres.

C A cross-section of a hedge and ditch

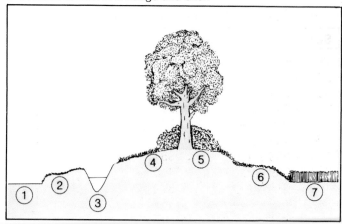

F Modern crop-spraying methods

65% of the labour force is provided by the farmers and their families and today there is only one permanent worker to every 240 acres compared with one to 74 acres in 1930. **)** (E)

Fertilisers are often used. There are sprays to kill both pests and weeds and this has led to a big increase in crop yield since 1945. **F** shows modern crop-spraying machinery being used. Chart **G** gives the increase in wheat production between 1957 and 1968, and **H** shows the size of modern farms.

G Wheat production 1957-1968

Year	Tons	Yield per acre (cwt)
1957	2 679 000	25.4
1960	2 988 000	28.5
1963	2 975 000	31.1
1966	3 415 000	30.6
1968	3 515 000	29.8

H Farm sizes in England and Wales 1970

Size	Number of Farms
¼ – 19 acres	135 657
20 – 49 acres	54 356
50 – 99 acres	53 119
100 – 149 acres	27 586
150 – 299 acres	31 740
300 – 499 acres	10 206
500 – 699 acres	2851
700 – 999 acres	1415
1000 acres +	862

?????????????????

1 a In **C**, match up points **1 – 7** with the following: road; ditch; verge; bank; crop; hedge; field edge.
b Why is Professor Hoskins so angry about the destruction of our hedges in **D**?
c Use **C** and **D** to work out the difference between a *hedge* and a *hedgebank*.
d If we continue losing 5000 miles of hedge a year, how many more miles of hedges can we expect to lose by the year 2084?

2 a Draw a line down the centre of your page. At the top of the left-hand column, write *Advantages of Hedges* and at the top of the right-hand column write *Disadvantages of Hedges*. Now write as many items in each column as you can.
(*Points to consider*: wind, machinery, wild-life, drainage, plants, timber, crop yields, space, cattle, the landscape, game-birds, shade, berries, maintenance, weeds, crop-burning, chemicals, rubbish, walkers.)
b On balance, do you think we need more or fewer hedges?

3 a Why was the 1947 Agriculture Act passed?
b A similar organization to the National Agricultural Advisory Service was set up in 1793. What was it called?
c According to **A**, what effect did the Act have on the numbers of farm labourers and working horses?

4 Imagine you are a hill farmer in Cumberland. It is January 1947. On the radio you hear that blizzard conditions are expected in your area within a few hours. You have about 200 sheep scattered over 50 square miles of hillside and moorland. Write an account of what happens to you on the night of 30 January 1947.

29 Down on the Factory Farm

❛ Oh, I am a battery hen,
On me back there's not a germ,
I never scratched a farmyard,
And I never pecked a worm,
I never had the sunshine
To warm me feathers through.
Eggs I lay. Every day.
For the likes of you.

But it's no life for a battery hen,
In me box I'm sat,
A funnel stuck out from the side,
Me pellets comes down that.
I gets a squirt of water,
Every half a day,
Watchin' with me beady eye
Me eggs roll away.

I might have been a farmyard hen,
Scratchin' in the sun,
There might have been a crowd of chicks,
After me to run.
There might have been a cockerel fine,
To pay us his respects,
Instead of sittin' here,
Till someone comes and wrings our necks. ❜ (A)

Pam Ayres

B Chickens in a battery unit

Today, with more and more people to feed, we have to produce more meat and dairy produce than ever before. To cope with this growing demand, agriculture has become *intensive*. This means that on many farms, animals are raised and looked after in the smallest space possible. Intensive breeding is sometimes known as 'factory farming'. **B** shows a battery unit where the chickens mentioned in **A** might have been kept.

In this battery unit thousands of hens are kept in wire cages. Their droppings fall through the wire onto a conveyor belt which carries them away. Another belt takes away their eggs which roll slowly out of their cages. By law, the cages have to be wide enough for the birds to be able to stretch out one wing. Another belt brings the hens their food. They live for eleven months and then most are killed off because they are riddled with disease. Some farmers buy them from the owners of the battery unit before they are killed off and let them roam around farmyards in a more natural way. They are then known as 'free range' hens. One Devon farmer who owns a smallholding near Cullompton said:

❛ I bought a few of these battery hens for a couple of quid. When I got them back to the farm, I found they could hardly walk at all. One bird kept losing its balance and falling over. A couple of them died. It took them ages to learn how to scrap (hunt around for food). ❜ (C)

D shows 'free range' birds.

Pigs are also kept in battery houses. These are similar in design to the hen houses, only bigger. The sows are kept in small groups inside the building with a sleeping area and a dunging area. When they are due to have piglets, they are put into narrow crates in which it is impossible for them to turn round. When the piglets are born, they are attracted away from the sow by an infra-red light as shown in **E**.

Other huts are used solely for fattening pigs. They have a long corridor down the middle of them with small compartments to either side. The fattening pigs are kept in the compartments except when the light is switched on for thirty minutes, twice a day, so that they can feed. They are kept in darkness so that they do not fight or move about and so lose weight. The temperature is kept very high.

D Free-range birds

Some farmers disagree with rearing animals like this. They say it is inhumane and unnatural to run a farm like a food factory. Other farmers argue that the animals enjoy clean, warm, hygienic conditions and that factory farming provides the public with plenty of cheap food. One farmer had this to say about thousands of chicks being reared in a huge 'broiler house':

❝ *No, I don't think it's cruel. The chicks are housed in a large, well insulated, well ventilated, well lit, superb dwelling. The chicks are plunged into darkness for 30 minutes a day so that they won't be alarmed when there is a power failure. All the equipment hangs from the ceiling. No floor space is wasted. I am quite satisfied there is no cruelty. The broiler chicken enjoys its life. It wouldn't grow if it didn't!* ❞ **(F)**

E The use of infra-red light to attract piglets from their mother

??????????????????

1 Find references in **A** that suggest:
 a that most battery hens are throttled after a period of time.
 b that battery hens live in cramped, confined conditions.
 c that a conveyor belt is used to take eggs away after they have been laid.
 d that battery hens are deprived of sunlight.
 e that food and water are fed to the hens automatically.

2 Contrast the conditions enjoyed by hens in **B** and **D**

3 **a** What arguments are used by the farmer in **F** to justify rearing chicks in a 'broiler house'?
 b Why do you think some farm workers prefer working on factory farms rather than on the more traditional types of farm?
 c How would you like to work in a battery unit like **B**?

4 The following statistics show the percentage of the laying flock kept on free range, battery cages or deep litter (keeping hens in a poultry shed on a 'deep litter' of straw or wood shavings):

	1960	1975
Free range	31%	3%
Battery	19%	93%
Deep litter	50%	4%

 a What sort of system was most widely used for keeping laying hens in 1960?
 b What change had taken place by 1975?
 c How do you account for this change?
 d List the advantages and disadvantages of each system.

30 The Future of Farming

In 1973 Britain, Eire and Denmark joined the European Economic Community (the EEC). The EEC is sometimes known as 'The Common Market'. The Community had been formed in 1957 by countries 1 – 6 in A. The aim had been to make trade easier between the six countries. It was believed that in this way a higher standard of living could be enjoyed by most Europeans. B shows the main events in Britain's negotiations to join the EEC, and C outlines the arguments for and against membership.

Soon Britain's entry into the EEC affected British agriculture and the price of food. The Community's policy towards agriculture is known as the Common Agricultural Policy (CAP). This states that no matter what happens to farm prices in Common Market countries, the prices received by the community's farmers will not be allowed to fall below a certain level. A system of subsidies ensures that European farmers receive a fair price for their goods. To protect farmers from foreign competition, a tax is placed on food being brought into Europe. At the same time, if prices in the EEC show signs of falling below a certain level, the Community buys up the produce at a fixed price.

A The European Economic Community in 1983

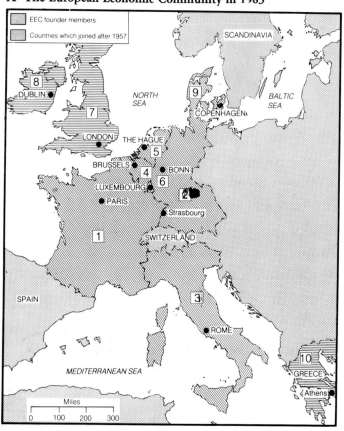

The effect of the CAP was that by the mid-1970s the price of food in Britain had gone up and certain items were being produced in too great a quantity. As farmers did not have to worry about competition from abroad, they could produce as much butter or wine as they liked, knowing that they would get a good price for their produce whatever happened.

Soon people were aware that there were 'butter mountains' and 'wine lakes' in the EEC as stocks rose. Some of the surplus was sold to countries like Russia at a very low price. The sale of EEC produce at a cheap rate to countries outside the Common Market attracted a lot of criticism.

In some parts of Europe, farming methods were old-fashioned and inefficient. Many farms were too small to use modern machinery. It became another goal of the CAP to increase the size of European farms. Sums of money were offered to uneconomic farmers to persuade them to give up their small farms. D shows farm sizes in the EEC in 1975.

It seems possible that Europe's farms will increase in size over the next few years. One farmer recently warned:

B Main events in Britain's campaign to join the Common Market

1957 *The Treaty of Rome* Six European countries, Belgium, France, West Germany, Italy, the Netherlands, Luxembourg form the European Economic Community (the EEC) under The Treaty of Rome. They agree to remove *tariffs* (taxes) on each other's goods

1959 *The Treaty of Stockholm* Britain and six other countries, Austria, Denmark, Norway, Portugal, Sweden and Switzerland form the European Free Trade Association (EFTA)

1961 Britain tries to join the EEC but no agreement reached

1963 Britain again tries to join EEC but France refuses to let Britain in

1967 French opposition again prevents Britain from joining EEC

1970 Fresh negotiations started between Britain and the EEC

1973 Britain, Denmark and Ireland become members of the EEC

1974 The Labour Party held a referendum to allow people a vote on Britain's membership of the EEC. 67.2% of the voters wanted to see Britain staying in the EEC

C Arguments for and against Britain's entry

Arguments in favour of joining EEC

1 Britain and EFTA unable to compete successfully with the EEC, so it was in Britain's best interests to join

2 Entry into the EEC would open up wider markets for Britain in Europe

3 More jobs would be created in farming and in industry; workers would be able to travel from country to country in search of jobs

4 It would mean a higher standard of living and cheaper food

5 It would eventually lead to a strong, united Europe

6 It would prevent European wars

Arguments against joining EEC

1 Entry into the EEC would weaken Britain's ties with the Commonwealth and the USA

2 Entry into the EEC would harm valuable trade with Scandinavia

3 It would lead to higher food prices and less efficient farming

4 It would damage Britain's agriculture and industries by harmful competition

5 It would lead to the loss of Britain's independence as a nation

6 The EEC was a 'rich man's club' in that it helped 'agribusinessmen' (businessmen who invest in farming) to make money by reducing tariffs

7 The EEC was an economic alliance of rich nations which largely ignored the needs of Third World countries like India and Pakistan.

‘In the future there will be no hedges or ditches, trees will either be huge forests or not at all, huge machines will crawl across the landscape but no human figure will ever be seen. Vast areas of the same crop will be grown. No animals or birds will be visible: domestic animals or birds will all be housed in enormous buildings and wild animals and birds will have died out, having had their natural habitat destroyed. **(E)**

On the other hand, there has been a drift back to the land from towns and cities in the 1960s and 1970s. Some people have set up small communities or co-operatives with the aim of achieving 'the good life' and becoming self-sufficient. There are many who believe that with the price of oil going up every year, a time will come when fewer machines will be used and alternative sources of power developed. Other farmers have taken an interest in organic farming — farming without chemicals or fertilisers. However, organic farming is labour-intensive (it requires more workers per acre than other types of farming) and food produced in this way is good to eat but expensive to buy.

No one can be sure what the future holds for farmers in Britain and the EEC. The only thing that we can be certain of is that as farming has changed a great deal since 1700, it is likely to change just as much over the next 200 years. If we can begin to understand some of these changes, it may give us some idea of patterns of change likely to occur between the present day and the next century.

??????????????????

1 In **A**:
a Identify countries 1 – 9.
b In which capital is the headquarters of the EEC?
c Name the country in central Europe which is *not* a member of the EEC.
d Which country or countries in **A** may soon apply for membership of the EEC?

2 Explain what these words and letters mean:
a surplus; b subsidy; c 'wine lake'; d EEC; e CAP.

3 Using **D**:
a Draw a block graph to show average farm sizes in EEC countries in 1975.
b Draw the farm sizes of the original six members of the EEC in one colour and the three later member states in another.
c Which country had the smallest average farm size in 1975?
d Which three countries had farms whose average size was about the same?
e Why do you think the average size of UK farms was so much greater than those in the rest of Europe?

4 Using **E** as a guide, *either* draw a picture entitled 'Landscape of the Future' *or* describe in detail what a 'bird's eye view of Europe' might look like in 1998.

5 *Either* describe a 'robot-controlled' farm of the future run by computers, machines and weird gadgets *or* write a story about a man who has a highly paid job in a city but who gives this up in order to start a self-sufficient smallholding in the countryside.

D Average farm sizes in EEC countries 1975

Country	Farm size (in hectares)
Belgium and Luxembourg	14
France	27
Italy	12
The Netherlands	14
West Germany	14
Denmark	21
Eire	18
United Kingdom	45

31 Quiz Time

Below are thirty questions about agriculture 1800-1980. The correct answers are printed at the bottom of the page — in the wrong order. Match up the questions and answers correctly.

1 Name the Act of Parliament passed in 1815 designed to restrict grain imports into Britain.

2 What is 'threshing'?

3 For what offence were the 'Tolpuddle Martyrs' prosecuted?

4 Name *two* leaders of the Anti-Corn Law League.

5 What natural disaster of 1846 led to the repeal of the Corn Laws?

6 When was 'The Golden Age of Farming'?

7 With what improvement in farming do you associate the name of Justus von Liebig?

8 Where was an important agricultural research station set up in 1842?

9 Who wrote a novel in 1886 which included a description of a seed drill?

10 With what sort of agricultural machinery do you associate McCormick?

11 Name two killer diseases affecting cattle and sheep between 1873 and 1879.

12 From which countries was meat brought into Britain during the 1870s?

13 What sort of farmers remained fairly well off right through 'The Great Depression'?

14 Name the agricultural labourer from Warwickshire who formed a farm-workers' union in 1872.

15 What do the initials NALU stand for?

16 What name is given to trade clubs set up to help workers in time of sickness or old age?

17 Name the committees set up in 1916 to bring more arable land under cultivation.

18 With what do you associate the name Fordson?

19 What is a U-boat?

20 Which Act was passed in 1931 to control farm prices and output?

21 Who invented a new type of milking machine in the 1930s?

22 Name two items controlled by marketing boards in the 1930s.

23 Which government department issued ration books in 1940?

24 What name was given to the women who worked on the land as part of the war effort 1940-1945?

25 Name the organization set up in 1947 to advise farmers about food production.

26 Which famous historian has criticized the destruction of our hedgerows?

27 What name is given to the units used to house factory-farmed chickens?

28 What name is used to describe chickens which are allowed to roam around farmyards in a 'natural' way?

29 What do the initials EEC stand for?

30 Which is the smallest country in the EEC?

Cobden and Bright
Luxembourg
Professor Hoskins
Thomas Hardy
Tractors
Agricultural Marketing Act
Irish Potato Famine
Rothamsted
War Agricultural Committees
Joseph Arch

German submarine
Shields
Hops, potatoes
Taking an illegal oath
European Economic Community
Friendly Societies
Ministry of Food
Women's Land Army
1840-1870
Batteries

Phosphates and fertilisers
National Agricultural Advisory Service
Dairy farmers
Free range
Corn Law
National Agricultural Labourers' Union
When grain is separated from straw
USA, Argentina, New Zealand
Liver rot, foot and mouth
Mechanical steam harvester